D1229949

BF   Nebel, Cecile.
411
.N42   The dark side of
1988   creativity

$18.50

DATE			

SOCIAL SCIENCES AND HISTORY DIVISION

THE CHICAGO PUBLIC LIBRARY
SOCIAL SCIENCES AND HISTORY DIVISION
400 NORTH FRANKLIN STREET
CHICAGO, ILLINOIS 60610

© THE BAKER & TAYLOR CO.

The Dark Side Of Creativity

The Dark Side of Creativity:

Blocks, Unfinished Works and
the Urge to Destroy

by

Cecile Nebel

The Whitston Publishing Company
Troy, New York
1988

SOCIAL SCIENCE & HISTORY DIVISION
EDUCATION & PHILOSOPHY SECTION

Copyright 1988
Cecile Nebel

Library of Congress Catalog Card Number 87-50837

ISBN 0-87875-346-X

Printed in the United States of America

671 86 249

To my family . . .

SOCIAL SCIENCE & HISTORY DIVISION
EDUCATION & PHILOSOPHY SECTION

Acknowledgments

It was a privilege to have excellent criticism, advice and suggestions from several colleagues, and I thank Professors Serge Hughes, Annette Insdorf, Cecile Insdorf, Pauline Kra, Jeanine P. Plottel and most especially Bettina L. Knapp and Michael Nimetz. I also thank Mr. Chris Miller for his help and invaluable editorial work and am deeply grateful to Trudy and Jean Nebel for their understanding and support.

Contents

Introduction

Artists have always destroyed their works. Self-doubt, a sense of impotence, anguish, inadequacy, uncertainty have more often than not accompanied artistic creativity. The urge to destroy comes about because somehow the work does not fulfill the ideal vision of its creator. Although artists rarely create according to a precise esthetic doctrine, they do, with some frequency, destroy their works because of dissatisfaction rooted in esthetic principles. It is clear that artists have other reasons as well for destructive urges involving themselves and their works, as a growing number of psychological studies attest. This book considers the motives which lead artists to despair of and destroy their work.

Such acts of destruction or abandonment of an unfinished work, involve a host of diverse, sometimes unrelated and often contradictory motivations. Consideration of these actions can bring us some insight into the difficulties and obstacles faced by the artist and his ways of overcoming them. The creative process, so often accompanied by acts of destruction, may affect the artist's approach to future works. A work, finished or not, produces in many artists an aftershock ("choc en retour") of one type or another. As a result, artists are led to reflect upon the work, to change, to modify, and even on occasion to destroy it. The interplay of these factors is the subject of this study.

A work which delights and enriches the amateur or connoisseur may have no such effect on its creator, but may rather torment him, both while he is creating it and—more often than not—after he has "finished" it. In addition to his own dissatisfaction, the artist's lot, as André Malraux pointed out, is to reject the forms created by others. This is the only way he has not only of becoming master in his own house, but often of becoming an artist at all. The creative instinct or urge proceeds in part from the need to reject, but this need only arises after an artist has known the works of others and felt the desire to challenge and surpass them.[1] To what extent this theory can ever be proven remains an interesting question, but there are several examples which suggest that it contains a great deal of truth. The painter Manessier charmingly told an interviewer:

> And also one has a lot of people in the studio: the great old masters, the geniuses: Rembrandt, Goya, Delacroix . . . You have to throw them out, show them the door. It isn't easy, they come back.[2]

The tormented nature of the relationship between the artist and his work has led psychologists and others to conclude that many creators suffer from an obsessional neurosis. The psychologist Robert Frances summarized the ideas of his colleague Pickford who noted such a condition in Cézanne.[3] He claimed that among its symptoms were slow maturation of each canvas, attention given to the smallest details, compulsion to treat the same theme and, above all, constant self-criticism. This description fits not only Cézanne but many other artists, and it is hard to believe that there could exist any who do not exhibit most of these traits. Self-criticism is a built-in feature of the artistic personality; it is found among artists of all times and all places.[4] Studying this dissatisfaction and its causes can help us to understand the "neurosis" without which there would probably be no artists at all.

This study begins with a short introductory chapter concerning theoretical issues that most artists grapple with at one time or another, and that often lead them to abandon or destroy their work. The second chapter deals with three writers,—Gustave Flaubert, Marcel Proust's narrator, and Roger Martin du Gard—who exemplify the throes of creative work; the third chapter, with three artists—William Wordsworth, Robert Musil and Arrigo Boito—who could not finish works on which they spent from twenty-five to fifty years. In the last chapter I have attempted to show the reasons which led Claude Monet, Paul Cézanne, Franz Kafka, Paul Dukas, Georges Rouault, Chaim Soutine and Alberto Giacometti to destroy completed or nearly completed works. This chapter also deals with Sigmund Freud, who, on several occasions, destroyed his notebooks, manuscripts and letters.

An inquiry of this kind is inevitably limited, if only because of the lack of source material available. Pertinent information can only come from artist's autobiographies, letters, diaries, or the testimony of well-informed witnesses. Such materials are rarely, if ever, available before the late eighteenth century. Even when they exist they are less than helpful because they are fragmentary, vague and not to the point. It is mostly for nineteenth and twentieth centuries artists that enough source material is available. Before this time, artists were loath to write about works they had destroyed and seemed reluctant to publicize what might be construed as their failures.

Artists often incorporate parts of destroyed works into subsequent ones and do not consider the destruction to be total. The contemporary American painter Lee Krasner, for example, told an interviewer that "she has always destroyed a good deal of her work, often bringing it back in other forms."[5] Artists have always recast works, with the same material reappearing in one form after another and therefore did not experience blockages, discouragement and a sense of having failed as overly traumatizing.

Since the end of the nineteenth century artists have been much more open about their sense of failure and helplessness, their anguish, doubts and torments, than ever before. It may be that this openness is a result of the breakthroughs made by Freud and other psychoanalysts. It is known that some artists, including Mahler, Rachmaninoff, Musil and Anais Nin, consulted psychoanalysts for help in overcoming their sense of anguish or of failure.

Artists who abandon or destroy works do so for a variety of reasons peculiar to their own personal situations. The problem of each individual must be looked into in some detail; no general laws or theories can adequately explain them all. It seems, however, that in most cases, artists have blocks and destroy their work because they cannot overcome doubts about its value and their originality.

Notes

1 André Malraux, *Les Voix du silence* (Paris: Gallimard, 1951), pp. 308, 337, 346.

2 Jean Clay, *Visages de l'art moderne* (Lausanne: Editions Rencontre, 1969), p. 245.

3 Robert Frances, *Psychologie de l'esthétique* (Paris: Presses Universitaires de France, 1968), p. 164.

4 M. D. Phillippe, *L'Activité artistique.   Philosophie du faire.*   2 vols. (Paris: Beauchesne, 1969, 1970).   See Chapter VIII of volume I for a detailed list of artists who have shown themselves to be very dissatisfied with their work.

5 Grace Glueck, "Scenes from a marriage: Krasner and Pollock," *Art News*, December 1981, p. 61.

A Theoretical View

The question of imagination plays a crucial role in the artist's view of his works. There are differences in the ways that artists understand the meaning of the word "imagination." Both Vasari and Condivi (Michelangelo's official biographier, to whom the artist virtually dictated his text) wrote that the master's imagination was so great, so powerful that he was not able to execute the work as he had seen it in his mind's eye. The frustration that resulted made him so unhappy that, according to Vasari, the sculptor would have sold few if any of his works had not financial necessity forced him to do so. In writing this, Vasari claimed to be quoting Michelangelo himself. The latter's frustration must have been in direct proportion to the grandeur of what he had imagined.

One cannot help but speculate that if Michelangelo had little esteem for his own work, he must have felt isolated and misunderstood by those who praised it, for they had no way of knowing that his work was not what he had envisioned. It seems doubtful that he could have set much store on the praise of his admirers; they most probably didn't know what they were talking about.

Whether there were in fact any persons whose artistic judgment and appreciation Michelangelo trusted is not clear. To be sure, he never lacked patrons and admirers: he was much sought after by four successive popes and many noblemen, and was highly praised in his own lifetime. But he did not seem to have a close relationship with any particular friends or patrons with whom he could discuss his esthetic ideas or problems concerning his work. Valéry wrote than when an artist cannot rely on the judgment and criticism of people he knows to be trustworthy, he feels his isolation all the more. He lamented the disappearance of connoisseurs whose understanding endowed the work of art with real value. He noted that "they were passionate and incorruptible judges for whom or against whom it was wonderful to work." He felt that a creation was a partnership or a cooperative effort between the amateur and the creator (he was even to write that it isn't the artist who creates a masterpiece, it is really the public).[1]   Michelangelo does not seem to have known any of these impassioned yet impartial observers.

In the case of Leonardo, both Vasari (1511-1574) and the theoretician Lomazzo (1538-1600), reported that when the master painted, he appeared to be hindered by the fear of not being able to execute his ideas, as his mind was filled with "the sublimity of art." Vasari specifically stated that despite Leonardo's enormous skill and mastery of his art, he could not finish works he had undertaken because he had formed in his imagination concepts that were too perfect. Since Vasari's "Life of Leonardo" appeared in 1550 (revised in 1568) and Lomazzo wrote in 1584—thirty one and sixty five years after the painter's death respectively—it is not clear whether their information is very accurate in all respects or whether they were adding to the legend which surrounded Leonardo even in his own lifetime. Much of Vasari's information came from the Anonimo Gaddiano, a perhaps sometimes unreliable biography of Leonardo and other painters written between 1537 and 1542. Concerning the painter Pontormo, Vasari stated that this artist's thought was so profound that it prevented him from painting, and that he died very much dissatisfied with himself for having been unable to fulfill his ideal.

Artists can also, of course, be unable to execute a work because of lack of imagination. Mallarmé's early poems often deal with the theme of sterility and impotence in art. This theme is evident in poems such as "Renouveau," "Angoisse," "Las de l'amer repos," "Le Sonneur," "L'Azur," "Brise marine," "Aumône," "Don du poème." But this sense of sterility was displaced by the idea of writing what Mallarmé called Le Livre, a book encompassing his total vision. In a letter to Verlaine, written in 1885, he stated that while he would never be able to write this book, his goal was to create at least a fragment of it, so that by its proportions the reader would have an idea of the work it was to have been part of.

Mallarmé's statement recalls an observation by Vasari, who wrote that although Michelangelo's Medici Madonna was unfinished and showed chisel marks, one could perceive the perfection of the completed work. In his Michelangelo, Herbert von Einem pointed out that often enough an artist realizes that a work cannot be completed, that he has reached the limit of what he can achieve. He must then let the work stand as is and hope the public will see in it both the beauty it contains and the one it foreshadows.[2]

Many artists who agonize over every note, brushstroke or word (like Flaubert), are searching for a perfection they suspect is unattainable. Ending a work provides a new and special source of anguish and often, for a great many artists, this act does not mean that the work is accomplished, whole or perfect. To them, finishing a work means simply that they themselves cannot do any more to it. Von Einem's statement about Michelangelo's difficulties in the matter of ending a work applies to many artists. Delacroix, for instance, noted in his *Journal* that to finish a work one needed a heart of steel, as decisions had to be made on everything. He was accustomed to encountering suddenly, and at every turn, difficulties he had never foreseen, so that whole works had to be reconsidered and were once again put in question. He felt that at such moments an artist's weaknesses appeared in full light and that what others call a finished work contains incomplete and uncompletable parts.[3]

Often artists reach a point when their own work becomes so alien, so closed that they must abandon it whether it is finished or not. In such instances, they may put it away without knowing what to do about it after having spent considerable time and effort on it. The problem of the alienation of the artist from his work also occurs upon its completion. M. D. Philippe quotes a passage by the poet Pierre Emmanuel who explained that once a work was finished he felt a stranger to it, exiled from it—feelings accompanied by a nostalgia for the work mixed with the "Luciferian taste of nothingness."[4] What was everything to him was now gone, to such an extent that he thought he had lost his identity and would be able to regain it only by forgetting himself in a new poetic creation.

For every artist who reacts to the finished work in this way, there is another who sees in it his identity, who sees himself in the mirror that the work constitutes, and who sees himself in this mirror just as he is, with all his limits.[5] It is often the dissatisfaction and unhappiness he feels at seeing these limits which motivate the artist to undertake another work where these can be transcended. Some artists are extremely reluctant to part with their work and feel the need to rework it, even when, in the case of a painting, it hangs in a museum. Bonnard went to museums, brush and can of paint in hand, to retouch his paintings.[6]   Valéry reported that Degas asked collectors who owned his works to let him take these back to his studio where he intended to make some changes. At least once, he completely ruined a pastel and the collector Rouart took to hiding Degas' paintings when the latter was invited to dinner.[7]

Pierre Schneider comments that this kind of behavior can be explained by the fact that artists such as Bonnard, Turner and Degas felt that a lifegiving relationship existed between themselves and their work. They were not motivated by a desire to reach perfection, which they knew was impossible, but rather they attempted to prolong the sustaining or enriching experience through creativity.[8]

For many artists, the product is of much less interest than the opportunity to solve problems, to overcome obstacles, to test their skills and abilities. As Valéry put it, the artist's goal is, in fashioning an object, to mold himself into what he wants to become: "Faire c'est se faire."[9]   The art critic Harold Rosenberg quoted Paul Klee as saying: "The work of art is primarily creation; it is never experienced as mere product" and he himself added: "The work is identical with the movement, psychological and manual, that created it. When the movement stops, the work is done."[10]   It is understandable that artists have difficulty ending such a symbiotic relationship with their work. If Rosenberg's statement is correct, there is a direct connection between the artist's movement or gesture and his work, so that understanding the artist leads to understanding the work—something many people believe to be clearly visible in painting and specifically in action painting.

The poet and critic Alfred Alvarez has remarked that we are living in a time when the work of art is not free-standing or autonomous. It was felt to be autonomous by many writers and critics at various times during the nineteenth and twentieth centuries. Alvarez, like Rosenberg, believes it is now dependent entirely on the psychological and emotional sources of its creation and reflects them quite clearly. Both critics feel that the work mirrors, fixes but does not transcend the "energy, appetites, moods and confusions of experience" that went into it.[11]   Many regret the passing of the era of Olympian detachment on the part of artists, when a sound understanding of a work was possible even when nothing was known of its creator, when knowledge of the author's life added nothing to our understanding of his work. As if somehow anticipating the objections of such criticism, Rosenberg wrote: "In the art of our time, the identity of the artist is a paramount theme."[12] He added that this led the artist to involve himself in such a way as to leave on the canvas traces of the activities and processes he went through in creating it. This is particularly noticeable in the case of sculptors and of abstract expressionist and action painters. The painter and sculptor are present in the work in the sense that their hesitations, gestures, movements and energy are there for anyone to see.

In contrast, Michelangelo destroyed drawings and sketches for fear that posterity would see works done when he was not at his best; he was anxious to efface the gropings which led to the finished work. More recently, Valéry aimed at a process of creation which would be as elegant, as perfect and free flowing as the final work (*Cahiers*, XVIII, 560). But the artist's identity is so prominent in modern art and so much importance is placed on the creative process that the work itself is now of secondary importance. Rosenberg believed that it was for this reason that many artists created paintings and sculptures out of rapidly disintegrating materials. He quoted Duchamp as saying that the use of such materials was "the most revolutionary attitude possible because they know they're killing themselves by using perishable materials."[13] It is as if Duchamp, the Swiss-born sculptor Jean Tinguely (born in 1925) and others had lost faith in the very possibility of painting and sculpture, in the existence of art itself, in creating coherent and durable forms. Although this faith was gone, any proof that they were right somehow shocked these artists and caused them surprising unhappiness. They no longer attach much importance to the work or its value, and emphasize the creative process and its effect on the viewer. When the effect wears off, since the work has no other content, there is nothing in it to hold anyone's interest and the work is burnt out—and its creator with it.

Artists like Duchamp and Tinguely do not have the same confidence in art that Monet and the Impressionists had. Monet's idea of art was still a traditional one of belief in the intrinsic value of the work as product, regardless of the identity of its creator. Duchamp, Tinguely and the abstract expressionists believe more in the work of art as process than as product. Interestingly enough, it was the Impressionists who first had the idea that the manner in which the work was created was at least as important as the product itself. Manet expressed the Impressionist credo, however unwittingly, when he said: "There is only one true thing: to do on first attempt what you have seen."[14]

A statement such as this indicates the artist's awareness that time is a major factor in the art of painting; it implies the idea of making a series of paintings, each showing a specific moment in time, thus giving enormous importance to the instant, to the fleeting moment to be captured before it vanishes. To do this, technique or the manner of painting is of the essence. While the Impressionists still attached great value to the product, the element of directness and spontaneity was of paramount importance as well as "the moment, psychological and manual, that creates the work."[15]   Manet's statement prefigures the series of paintings later done by Monet who was reluctant to part with any one of them until the whole series was finished, as each canvas could only be understood and judged in the context of the entire series. Artists have always felt that making something eternal of the transitory was one of the functions of art. But the Impressionists' attempt at depicting the ephemeral, the very texture of instants of time, was done for the enjoyment of an ephemeral beauty as if the painters had little illusion about fixing forever on their canvas a beauty so changeable in itself that it would have been folly to think it transcended time.

Impressionism, as is well known, provoked very strong reactions, and Cézanne, while he did not reject the techniques of the Impressionists, was interested in an art that would go beyond capturing mere appearance and changing beauty. He wanted to make of Impressionism something "solid like the paintings in the museums."[16]   Many people have felt that his art was a defense against the dispersion of the appearance of things: "Everything we see is dispersed and disappears. Nature is always the same but nothings remains of it, nothing of what we see." Feeling more anxious about the instability of nature than many other painters of his time, Cézanne told Gasquet: "Our art must give it (Nature) the shimmer of its duration with the elements, the appearance of all its changes. It must make us feel Nature's eter-nity."[17]

Clearly, a revolution in attitudes took place between Cézanne's time and Duchamp's. The latter's attitude toward art is quite the opposite of the one Malraux attributed to modern artists. For this novelist the question of an artist's self-confidence is of such importance that it shapes his behavior. He believed that Monet, at the height of his glory, was filled with anguish when he lost confidence in his painting and added that no master of today could live with the certainty that his work would not survive him.[18]   He also remarked that artists' lack of confidence in their work and its value would inevitably lead them to destroy their creations.   But there is no evidence that artists who believed their work would not survive them or not survive them long, destroyed it with any greater frequency than those who didn't suffer from this doubt.   More often than not, artists fear that their work will survive, and they destroy what they judge to be inferior.   This is precisely what Monet did on the numerous occasions when he burned hundreds of canvases.[19]

In contrast to artists who have in their mind's eye a vision of what they want to achieve (a vision such as Vasari claimed Leonard, Michelangelo and Pontormo had) and also in contrast to the Impressionists whose aim was "to do on first attempt what one sees," other artists have felt that imagination is like a subterranean source from which fantasies, impulses and emotions pour forth quite unexpectedly.   The artist must allow this flow into his consciousness without repressing anything; he will then sort, examine, arrange these impulses to create a work of art, since what has poured forth from this hidden, inner source cannot be used in its raw state.   Many people do not believe in the possibility that material from the hidden source can flow into our consciousness.   Valéry wrote:

> No one has ever known how to, been able to, dared to write everything that comes to mind, and even more, we do not know how to think, to form in the mind itself, everything that sketches itself or could be; something in us, before us, chooses, eliminates, paralyzes what is possible (*Cahiers* XXI, 181).

Since there is a built-in repressive factor at work in us, it is often necessary to stimulate the imagination from the outside, although presumably the artist can attempt to get at repressed elements through a free association technique of the type used in psychoanalysis.   Even with the use of such a technique, he might not succeed in his efforts, or might feel that something is resisting him and experience dissatisfaction as well as a sense of failure.

Other artists have thought of the imagination as the ability to conjure up in their mind a vision of which they then tried to give form in a work of art.   Plotinus, for instance, wrote that art is "the realization of an inner concept," and Vasari evidently believed that the realization of such a concept was what Leonardo, Michelangelo and Pontormo tried to bring about.[20] Since he thought the concepts they had were too grandiose, they could not possibly be given form. The existence of conceptual prefiguration in the artist's mind has been denied by many, including Valéry, Merleau-Ponty, and Michel Butor. Valéry insisted that a work of art is never the result of the execution of an idea distinct from it (*Cahiers* XV, 63). Yet Leonardo's own notes contain the statement that the artist must give visible form to the idea and invention which first exists in his imagination.   This implies a belief that the artist has in his imagination a concept or image of what he wants to do. It could be that Leonardo made this statement to impress upon his pupils or other painters that one must accumulate sketches and drawings before starting on the painting itself.

The idea of a concept of a work preexisting in the artist's imagination can cause no end of difficulty, as those who believe in such a concept blame themselves for not achieving what they expect to—even when such expectations are entirely unrealistic and even impossible. If Vasari was correct in speculating that Leonardo's hand was paralyzed by his fear of not being able to create what he had envisioned, then this paralysis was the result of a wrong and harmful idea he held about an inner concept existing in his imagination. Lomazzo stated that Leonardo was only too ready to see faults in his paintings while others considered them to be miraculous creations. Etienne Gilson's comment that even with thorough and intense preparation, the artist still cannot know what his work will be, probably summarizes this situation very accurately, as does Valéry's sentence that the work of art is never the result of the execution of an idea distinct from it.[21] There are obviously too many imponderables in the act of executing on canvas, in stone or on paper what has been prepared in sketching, drawing or writing.

Many artists believe in Platonist fashion that any vision becomes flawed by taking on a form. This idea was summed up by the seventeenth century French Jesuit critic, Rapin: "There is nothing born into this world which does not distance itself from the perfection of its idea when coming into it."[22] It is difficult to know whether artists have an inner concept of the work when they begin it because the word "concept" is so vague. If it is taken to mean thought, idea, opinion or plan, then it is evident that no such thing exists in detail in the mind of the artist prior to the execution of the work. Artists are rather in a propitious frame of mind, or feel a disposition, emotion, impression, enthusiasm, attraction toward color, line, movement, rhythm, texture; they may have a vision of what they would like to create but it is too elusive to be called a concept.[23]

The question of knowing if an inner "concetto," to use the term prevalent during the Renaissance, is present before the artist's use of a model or whether it arises after he has been inspired by one, remains unanswered; the problem of what artists mean by "imagination" comes up in this connection. Are they working with elements completely invented or imagined, or with some element based partly on a model or on experience and partly invented? Balzac claimed that artists often have a gift of what he called "second sight," enabling them to imagine, feel, understand and create the real even before they experience it or live it.[24] Yet at another time he wrote that imagination can never equal the reality of the truth hidden in the lives of people living in large cities, and added that one finds there admirable scenes, tragic and comic, created by pure chance, which produce masterpieces the artist might well envy.[25] His statement to the effect that French society of his time was to be the model, and he the secretary who would transcribe what he had witnessed, is another case of the artist playing down the role of imagination and representing himself as a reporter who impartially sets down the truth.

An artist with a problem similar to Leonardo's is the subject of Balzac's short story "The Unknown Masterpiece." Balzac appears not to have read Vasari (none of the scholars who have exhaustively analyzed the story mention this source), but his character Frenhofer faces most of the problems which, according to Vasari, troubled Leonardo da Vinci. Like the latter, Frenhofer has an intuition of perfection to which he had trouble giving form. Every time he puts something down on the canvas, it is less than he expects or something other that he aims at, and he is too conscious of the gap between what he does and what he wants to achieve. Frenhofer himself claims that reality has not furnished him with the model he needs. He evidently has to take bits and pieces from here and there and fuse them into an organic whole whose parts seem to be joined harmoniously so that the effect would not be that of a piecemeal assemblage. Balzac's own opinion of Frenhofer's total failure, leading as it does to the destruction of all his paintings and to his suicide, is that the artist is never in on the secret of his creativity and is rather something like a medium for it.   Consequently, time spent in theorizing about art or criticizing one's work is wasted and diverts energy from its proper course.

Artists differ widely in their ideas of how much of their work is invention and how much is reaction to a stimulus provided by a model. George Sand spoke of three quarters invention in her work, yet she wrote to a young correspondent and aspiring writer that to be a great poet, one must have lived, felt, learned, meditated and suffered much more than he could possibly have done as he was still very young.[26] These different statements imply that the writer must have both experience of life and ability to invent and imagine.

In the same way, the narrator of *Remembrance of Things Past* wondered how he would ever be a writer as he had nothing of intellectual import to say, and common experience or ordinary emotions seemed to him totally unsuitable as the raw material from which books are made. With time, he would discover that it is with just such ordinary material that books are, in fact, made and on the day of the Guermantes party the much older narrator understands that he had to live his life before realizing it was to be the subject of his book. Yet in a 1913 letter to Madame de Noailles, Proust remarked that reality is not solid enough stuff and cannot match our dreams, implying that imagination has the principal role. The narrator states that art is a very delicate balance of reality and imagination which each artist must arrive at for himself. The solutions of others are not of much use to him. Many artists have insisted that even if there were such a thing as a concept in the artist's mind, it would be of little use to him. Valéry stated that "one finds the idea at the same time as one loses it in the work" (*Cahiers* XV, 63).

Proust's narrator noted that the writer's terrain, like the one on which battles are fought, reveals unexpected resources—impasses which cause him to deviate from a preconceived plan. Balzac's Frenhofer, the protagonist of "The Unknown Masterpiece," worked for ten years on a portrait of a beautiful young woman but apparently never had a model—or at least Balzac never made any mention of one or even of several—from whom Frenhofer could have copied different features. The old painter claimed that he could not finish his picture because he had never seen an irreproachable model, and said that he would give his entire fortune to see for one moment the ideal he was looking for. He could not find one either in reality or in his imagination. If he could not finish his work without a model with which to compare his creation, then the concept he had was not sufficient. Too preoccupied with theories, with reasoning—also because he lived too long with his work, felt it too intensely and did not work with a real model—Frenhofer, like many other of Balzac's fictional artists, became a monomaniac obsessed with his ideas, shut up in a world of his own. He proved that no concept is adequate without reality as a basis to support it.[28] Poor Frenhofer was not cut from the same cloth as Raphael, who wrote that, to paint the portrait of a beautiful woman, he would have to see many of them, but since there are so few he used "a certain idea which comes to my mind."[29]

Frenhofer was a victim of what Balzac called the over-abundance of the creative principle or the excessive power of the imagination.[30] Another of Balzac's artists, also showing a super-abundance of creative passion, made a beautiful statue of a nude woman, inspired by a model who did not pose for him but whose performance as a singer he watched every night at the opera; he did not know this singer was a castrato. The sculptor Sarrasine sees in this cantatrice a model he never imagined possible, one whose perfection inspires him to create a great work. He thinks the model is "more than a woman, it was a masterpiece, like Pygmalion's statue descended for him from her pedestal." The sculptor sketches, draws and sculpts from memory for ten days until he finishes the statue. When he finds out the truth about La Zambinella, Sarrasine is horrified, enraged and distraught; he bitterly denounces his inspirator, reproaching the singer for, among other things, not equalling his creation. He calls the statue "an illusion" and in a fit of anger tries, unsuccessfully, to destroy it because his pride and happiness are shattered. He has been deceived, but invested in his creation so much mental and emotional energy that when he understands the model was not equal to the work he has created or to his love for the woman he believed La Zambinella to be, he says—when stabbed by hired killers—that death is the best thing that can happen to him.

It is interesting that he called the statue an illusion, as he obviously felt, like Frenhofer, that there ought to exist an adequate correlation between the model and statue, i. e. between the model or person represented and the statue as representation. If this correlation does not exist, then there is a deception, a falsehood. Both Frenhofer and Sarrasine throw themselves into their work with such passion that they hardly need a model. Both are so absorbed by a vision or inner image that they lose touch with reality, only to be brought back to it, with tragic results. While Frenhofer's work does not measure up successfully to reality, in Sarrasine's case it is the model who does not equal the sculptor's creation. The story of both the painter and the sculptor brings to mind a famous statement by Keats: "Byron describes what he sees, I describe what I imagine. Mine is the hardest task" (Letter of 18 September 1819). This statement summarizes a feeling quite common among artists who have often believed that the imaginary is infinitely more difficult to give form to than the real, and that the imagined is always richer, more profuse, more satisfying than reality. This is undoubtedly one of the meanings of "Heard melodies are sweet, but those unheard/are sweeter."

Many artists besides Keats have felt that as soon as the imagined is given form, it loses its richness; form is reductive, imprisoning the expansive, protean quality of the imagined. Balzac's Sarrasine is proof of the fact that a model may fail to make the artist's task any easier, if only because the model does not match his ideal vision. Artists who habitually used models in describing the world outside them, or the inner nature of man, did not find their task any easier. Their aim was to define, analyze and express with clarity and concision—at the cost of great hardship—and this they considered the true purpose of art. Such artists very often distrusted imagination because they believed it invented or conjured up from the recesses of the mind the fantastic, the chimerical, the nonexistent, the unreal or untruthful. They did not think it was the artist's task to invent the unknown and did not put much stock in the view that people come to see the world in a new way precisely because of a vision imposed by an original artist. One thinks of Boileau's statement that a new idea is not one that nobody has ever had before; rather it is one we all have had—but the artist succeeds in expressing it better than ever before. La Bruyère and Flaubert both thought that everything had already been said.[31]

The idea that the original artist changes our view of things is one that was dear to the Romantics and to Proust, whose narrator writes that it was only after Renoir exhibited his canvases that people began to see reality as resembling the representations of this painter.[32] This is also what Wilde had in mind when he quipped that nature imitates art. Balzac wrote more than once that the artist's genius is precisely to create, invent, imagine what does not exist—what he has not yet known or experienced—but will exist and be experienced by himself and others once he has given form to the imaginary. Paradoxically enough, the painter Rouault believed that the more imagination an artist has, the more he has to be a realist, and develop gifts of observation to help him store up forms and harmonies so he can know reality better and find it more malleable.[33]   Rouault and Flaubert before him both believed that there is no contradiction between imagination and accurate description of reality.

At one point or another, most artists have faced the problem of the use of a model, and Roger Bordier in *L'Objet contre l'art* points out that the attitude of artists toward the model has always been "ambivalent, tormented and contradictory."[34] Pierre Bonnard (1867-1947) believed that a painter starts with an idea, and he considered it dangerous to rely on a model while painting. If he looks at a model the artist can lose his first idea, which should lead to the universal. If this "universal" or concept was lost, the painter would be bogged down in the depiction of the "particular" represented by the model. He would then no longer be master of his work, having abandoned the organizing idea he started with. Kandinsky, not surprisingly, felt that objects must be eliminated as they constituted obstacles.[35]

Abstract painters do not, of course, face the problem of the use of a model in the same way as do figurative painters. Bissière said that he usually began a painting with a sensation of color or an emotion. Once the first color has been put down on canvas, it calls forth another until the colors suggest a form.[36] Many non-figurative artists, of whom Arp was a good example, have stated that they have no preconceived idea when they begin a work, and that they may combine the occasional use of a model of some sort with the process, described by Bissière, of the imaginative response to colors in a sort of emotional chain reaction.

Prior to the advent of non-figurative art, critics probably insisted too often that the artist's objective was to reproduce the truth of reality, whether external or internal. To do this, in their view, artists had to copy a model, or synthesize and extrapolate by reproducing the best or truest elements of many models. But artists did not believe this and at times felt that such views led to their being completely misunderstood. George Sand wrote to Balzac that in a novel one neither wanted to copy a living model nor was able to, and she added that for better or worse three quarters of her characters were invented. She claimed that the public was foolish to want to recognize in the artist's creation the persons it thought had been the artist's models.[37] This is only one example of a writer lamenting the way the public limited a novelist's scope by insisting on find keys or models to explain a work not primarily based on a model. It is interesting that George Sand insisted that three quarters of her work was pure invention, as she worked in a genre where it had always been assumed that representation of reality is of the essence.

The question of whether or not artists should work from models was complicated by the fact that prior to the twentieth century, most writers, painters and sculptors did work from models—or so it was very widely assumed. Statements like the one attributed by Vasari to Leonardo (to the effect that he couldn't paint the faces of Christ and Judas in *The Last Supper* because he could not find any models or imagine what such faces could be like) only reinforce the impression that painters, sculptors, and by extension other artists as well, could not work without models. Very often, artists stated that they begin with some *données* which impress them and go on from there. The problem is to try to delimit the role of these *données* and that of the imagined element. The words "model" and "pattern" have a similar meaning, indicating something the artist notices in the world outside, or even inside himself, or a configuration he imposes on experience because of his attitudes, character or vision, and sensibility. Words like "model" and "pattern" thus refer to a complex situation in which one finds a mixture, in various degrees, of impressions, sensations, emotions, hypotheses, observation, understanding, judgment and a host of other conscious or unconscious reactions in which the artist's sensibility plays a very large part. It is evident that the imagination of Impressionist painters, for example, was very different from that of their predecessors as they are said to have painted not what they knew but what they saw. To paint in this way meant, of course, that their attitudes were quite different from their predecessors' and even from most of their contemporaries.

André Malraux contends that an artist begins by copying the work of others (their work serves as his model) and that he later asserts himself by rejecting the forms elaborated by his predecessors; according to Malraux, the artist does this whether or not he is conscious of it. Flaubert adds an interesting formulation to the models-versus-imagination debate when he writes that genius is the ability to work from an imaginary model who poses before you. He thought that when one saw it clearly it was possible to reproduce it.[38] He adds that whatever is totally imagined has an uncanny way of later becoming real, of being felt by the artist himself in very concrete situations. He also notes that everything one invents is true (*Corr.* III, 291). Like Balzac, he thinks that the artist has a second sight and can know what does not yet exist but will come into being through his creation; this second sight is not based on a real model but on an imaginary one, and it is the artist who does the modelling—creating the imaginary model out of his instinct or insight.

From creating an imaginary model to creating with no model at all was a step Flaubert himself wanted to take, as is clear from one of the most famous passages in his correspondence. He speaks of creating a work about nothing, with almost no subject, or in which the subject would be almost invisible (*Corr.* II, 345). Flaubert's wish turned out also to be that of the Impressionists who had begun painting in the late 1850's and 1860's. They worked from models, but it soon became evident that the model itself was of diminishing importance to them. Monet wrote that the subject is an insignificant thing and that what he wanted to paint was what was between himself and the subject of the painting, that what he wanted to paint was what he felt.[39] This aim prefigures the total disappearance of the model in modern art, whether in painting, sculpture or literature. Alain Robbe-Grillet has noted:

> The novelist's strength is precisely that he invents, he invents with complete freedom, without models. The modern narrative is remarkable in that it deliberately stresses this invention, to such a point that invention and imagination can even become the subject of the book.[40]

It is perfectly possible for a modern artist to take as the subject of his work the possibility or impossibility of giving form to what he has imagined, and this would cause the artist none of the frustration that artists experienced in the past. There is abundant evidence that many twentieth-century artists not only work without any preexisting concept but begin a work without any idea of what they are going to do. Among these artists, who have different reasons for adopting this practice, are Arp, Bazaine, Bissière, Carrade, Estève, Lapicque and Soulages.[41] This is now a perfectly common approach which has long ceased to cause any surprise; André Lhote contended that to know in advance what one is going to do merely disgusts the modern artist.[42] It is not only the model that has been abandoned but also the idea that the model of colors found in nature can be or should be imitated. Gustave Moreau wrote that without imagination it is impossible to create beautiful color, and that color must be thought, dreamed and imagined; such an opinion excludes any possibility of copying or imitating nature's colors.[43]

The German-born painter Ernst Ludwig Kirchner (1880-1938) held the same belief as Moreau and noted: " . . . color, too, is not born from nature, but from the painter's creative invention."[44]

The freedom to invent announced so confidently by Robbe-Grillet is, of course, an excellent thing for artists, but it seems highly doubtful that this freedom will lead them to face their work with greater confidence and serenity.

Generally, a time comes when artists wonder about their calling and feel the need to justify it, if only to themselves. At such moments they may recall the truism that everything has already been done. Invariably their answer to this could be put in the words of the sage Hillel: "If I don't do it, who will?" Since the middle of the eighteenth century, when originality became the essential factor that it still is, artists have realized that their only reason for being was to be themselves and to create a vision uniquely their own. The torment that most artists have experienced, the self-doubt, uncertainty, anguish and fear of not living up their ideal, is due in great part to the fear of failing to be authentically themselves. It is as if they had always known that the two most difficult things are those the philosophers summed up in the words: Know thyself and become who you are.

If an artist cannot believe in his own originality he may be led to destroy works because he misinterprets his strengths. This happened in the case of Kafka, whose famous letter to his father concerns the lack of support and understanding he had to contend with at home. He feared his own originality, he did not want to carry its burden and stated in the last years of his life that his art was an abyss, an immense void which would drag him down if he persisted in his compulsion to write. Soutine also manifested numerous signs of inferiority because he was unable to believe in the worth of what he had done. This is shown by his constantly seeking the approval of Madame Castaing and others, his inability to forget what critics had said about his early work, and his endless attempts to eradicate it.

The critic Monroe Beardsley's remark that originality is a standard for judging the composer and not the music is one that most artists would find very controversial.[45] Many artists of the nineteenth and twentieth centuries believed that their only *raison d'être* was to create as a means of self-discovery, self-knowledge, and the expression of a unique outlook. Those who did not believe in their originality felt that they had no foundation to stand on. They did not see any reason for their work unless it enabled them to explore and develop some aspect of their lives. In this exploration most felt that they contributed something because of their very individuality. It has also, of course, been the hope of artists that their work would interest, help, or benefit others. Yet without their belief in originality they would certainly not have gotten very far, especially in times when the Church and aristocracy no longer provided much patronage.

Many artists, whether they like it or not, have to admit that their individuality is reflected in their work, if only in the sense that the work reflects the artist's limitations. It is precisely because he feared this mirroring effect that Picasso told André Malraux: "A painter's worst enemy is style."[46] This statement shows his belief that style permits the viewer to recognize both the individuality and personal limitations of the artist. But if he did not have a distinctive style he would not have the individuality the public seeks. If the artist is a chameleon even to himself, he cannot be recognized as an individual.

Very often artists do not know that they have arrived at their own style nor how they have created it. They understand the necessity of ridding themselves of what is not singularly their own and realize the need to be in touch with their innermost instincts. But they are never sure that they have captured the instinctive, natural and spontaneous elements essential in the synthesis of their personal style until someone comes along to copy it. Gauguin should have felt flattered that others were copying his style, but of course he wasn't, and Cézanne continually feared imitators.

It frequently appears to artists that the elements constituting their originality have come forth without their conscious participation. They often do not understand how these elements organize themselves within their work. They do not feel that they know how to control and direct what makes up their style.

Many artists are not sure which if any of the elements of their art are really original. It often appears to the artist that what others call his originality is an amalgam of what he has seen around him and reacted to. Of course, a personal expression of what is "in the air" is valuable if it is deeply felt, sincere, significant, intense and marked by a very individual stamp. Matisse summarized the artist's plight when he said: "What is best in the Masters, their very *raison d'être*, is beyond them. Not understanding it, they cannot teach it."[47]

Before an artist can be original he must, of course, clear away everything that is conventional, habitual and taken for granted. This is what Flaubert explained to Maupassant when he read and criticized the younger man's work. He told the fledgling writer that it is always possible to look at a person or thing long and attentively enough to finally discover something no one had seen before. Such discoveries are possible because normally we do not really see but "use our eyes with the memory of what others have thought."[48]

It is one thing to look at an object or person long and hard enough to discover what no one had ever noticed; real originality is something different. Maupassant did not say whether Flaubert spoke to him of the way in which an artist's personal vision enables him to contribute what is uniquely his own. Perhaps Flaubert felt that just by looking hard and long one would see what no one had ever seen because each onlooker or artist is so unpredictably different from all others. But in speaking to Maupassant he does not seem to have made a distinction between the difference in the things looked at and the difference in those looking at them.

In the preface to *Pierre et Jean* Maupassant noted that a writer is incapable of becoming each of the beings he depicts in his novels. The most the writer can do is to ask himself: "If I were this character, how would I react in the situation facing him?" It is always himself that the artist represents in his works, according to Maupassant. He added that the writer should only aim at concealing this truth from the reader.

Both novelists held to the theory of the impersonality of the author. Both believed he should not be seen directly in his work. The difference was that the older man believed that the artist could get into the soul of another by sheer effort of the imagination. The younger man thought that the only thing it was possible to achieve was empathy. Flaubert thought it neces-

sary for the artist to forget himself and imagine himself in the skin of another being. His younger colleague denied the possibility of such metamorphoses.

The narrator of Proust's *Remembrance of Things Past* specifically claims what his two predecessors did not. He writes that the work of artists helps us to understand first others and then ourselves. He places enormous importance on originality when he states that we derive insights and understanding from works of art. The knowledge that art gives us can only be attributed to an artist's originality and his ability to *represent* in ways in which he differs from others. In "Religion and Literature" (1925), T. S. Eliot remarked that artists do not give us direct knowledge of life, and that readers must be aware enough to realize that the insights they derive from a work are worthwhile only because they come from someone they consciously know to be different from themselves.

Artists seem to know instinctively that originality is not an element one starts with or inevitably finds. Rather it is something one must create, discover, develop, or shape over a period of time. Often an artist fails to realize when he has "found his own voice": he is too involved in his work to step back and view it impartially. Cézanne, for example, complained that he had only "une petite sensation" and that Gauguin had stolen it from him. Even allowing for Cézanne's extreme wariness of others, one is at a loss to understand how the painter could have believed this for a moment. Cézanne's statement shows that he himself was not sure about his originality, nor fully aware of its nature and extent.

As for Gauguin, statements about his borrowings from Emile Bernard, Sérusier, Van Gogh and Cézanne had reached him in far-off Tahiti. He was extremely hurt by them, even though he knew they were largely without substance. His letter to Maurice Denis of June 1899 shows how badly he felt about the accusations made against him on this score. In his reply to Denis' invitation to exhibit with his former friends, Gauguin used all the sarcasm and irony he could muster. He also thought, rightly or wrongly, due to remarks made by his correspondents, that others had begun to copy him. This was a particularly serious problem in his case as he depended on his style to sell paintings, and he had to sell in order to keep from starving. In a letter to his friend Daniel de Monfreid, he said of his imitators: "Ils font du Gauguin mais mieux." In other words, these imitators painted in his style better than he could.

For him, originality was an obsession. He indicated in a letter to Vincent Van Gogh's brother Théo that one of his reasons for wanting to leave France was that he thought the Far East had never had "its direct interpreter in Europe" and so would be a suitable subject for him.[49] At the end of his second stay in Tahiti, he wrote to the dealer Ambroise Vollard that he had "overdone Tahiti a little" and that going to live in the Marquesa Islands would be a stimulus for his work.[50]

Interestingly enough, it was Vollard who had written to Gauguin, at the end of 1899, that his paintings did not sell because they were "so different from what people are accustomed to."[51] To this the painter replied that the public "demands the greatest possible originality from a painter and yet will not accept him unless he resemble all the others."[52] He added, mockingly, that he did resemble those who imitated him. Vollard probably did not perceive or even care about the irony of this statement.

It certainly must have dawned on Gauguin that whatever he did at this time turned against him. He was doing work the public was not accustomed to, yet other artists imitated him to the point of producing pictures that look more like Gauguin than those of Gauguin himself. Cézanne deplored his bad influence.[53] Camille Pissaro had written to his son in 1893 that Gauguin always "poached" on other artists' turf and was now "pillaging the savages of Oceania."[54] It is a good thing Gauguin did not hear about Pissaro's opinion as it would have caused him much anguish; Vollard's comments had already seriously upset him. The painter must have wondered if he had the physical strength and moral courage to survive until such time as the public became accustomed to his painting; he knew that could take a long time. He had already attempted suicide in 1897. As it turned out, exhausted and desperately ill, he died four years after Vollard had written that Gauguin did not sell because of his extreme originality.

Artists who do not understand their originality and who torment themselves with thoughts of their inability to reach an inaccessible ideal have no way of breaking out of the vicious circle in which they are caught. Cézanne destroyed so many of his canvases because he did not understand his originality. Emile Bernard wrote that had he understood it, he would not have let his reasoning interfere with his work. But his will and his logic opposed his natural bent to such an extent that Cézanne himself often thought he would accomplish very little. Bernard noted that the great master did not lack artistic power but that he had pushed his thinking about his art too far. His theorizing about his art assumed too much importance; it dominated everything and nearly "paralyzed" his hand. Indeed, on more than one occasion Cézanne likened himself to the protagonist of Balzac's "The Unknown Masterpiece."[55]

The question of originality is one that artists encounter most often; it causes them great difficulties even when they do not consciously think about it. Their sense of its perplexities can be constraining. It affects their attitude toward themselves, their work and their judgment of it. This question is frequently the essential one shaping their life as artists—to many the only life that matters.

Notes

[1] Paul Valéry, *Oeuvres*, 2 vols. ed. Jean Hytier (Paris: Gallimard- -Pléiade, 1960), II, 1091.

[2] Herbert von Einem, *Michelangelo*, trans. Ronald Taylor (London: Methuen & Co., Ltd., 1973), pp. 257-259.

[3] Eugène Delacroix, *Journal*, 3 vols. (Paris: Plon, 1895), III, p. 426.

[4] see M. D. Philippe, *L'Activité artistique*, 2 vols. (Paris: Editions Beauchesne, 1969-1970), I, 359.

[5] Valéry, II, 673.

[6] Monroe Wheeler, *Bonnard and his environment* (New York: Doubleday, 1964), p. 20.

[7] Valéry II, 1232-1233.

[8] Pierre Schneider, *Louvre Dialogues* (New York: Atheneum, 1971), p. 5.

[9] Paul Valéry, *Cahiers*, 29 vols. (Paris: Centre National de la Recherche Scientifique (CNRS), 1957-1961), XXV, 619. All references to Valéry's *Cahiers* are to this edition.

[10] Harold Rosenberg, *The Anxious Object* (New York: Horizon Press, 1966), p. 99.

[11] Alfred Alvarez, *The Savage God* (New York: Random House, 1972), p. 255.

[12] Rosenberg, p. 100.

[13] Rosenberg, p. 91.

[14] Quoted in Antonin Proust, *Edouard Manet: Souvenirs* (Paris: Laurens,

1913), p. 30.

[15] Rosenberg, p. 91.

[16] Joachim Gasquet, *Cézanne* (Paris, 1921), p. 90.

[17] Gasquet, p. 80.

[18] André Malraux, *L'Intemporel* (Paris: Gallimard, 1976), p. 121.

[19] Lilla Cabot Perry, "Reminiscences of Claude Monet from 1889 to 1909," *The American Magazine of Art*, no. 3, March 1927, p. 119. Lilla Cabot Perry was a painter and Monet's neighbor at Giverny.

[20] Plotinus is quoted by Herbert von Einem, *Michelangelo*, p. 261.

[21] Gilson is quoted by Paul-Henri Michel, "The Lesson of the Renaissance," *Diogenes*, no. 46, 1964, p. 32.

[22] Quoted by Gérard Genette, *Figures* II (Paris: Editions du Seuil, 1969), 75.

[23] For a discussion of this question see Paul-Henri Michel, "The Lesson of the Renaissance," *Diogenes*, no. 46, 1964, pp. 25-43.

[24] See *La Comédie Humaine*, 12 vols. (Paris: Gallimard, Pléiade, 1976-1981). *Louis Lambert*, XI, 593. *La Peau de Chagrin*, X, 52.

[25] See *La Comédie Humaine*, *Facino Cane*, VI, 1020.

[26] George Sand, *Correspondance*, ed. Georges Lubin (Paris: Garnier, 1964—). See IV, 711 and VI, 481.

[27] For Proust's letter to Madame de Noailles see *Correspondance de Marcel Proust*, edited by Philip Kolb (Paris: Plon, 1976—). See vol. XII (1913), 74 and *A la recherche du temps perdu*, 3 vols. (Paris: Gallimard, Pléiade, 1954). See vol. III, 879. All references to Proust's correspondence and novel are to these two editions respectively.

[28] Balzac, "Des artistes," in *Oeuvres complètes*, 24 vols. (Paris: Club de l'Honnête Homme, 1956), XXII, 223.

[29] Quoted in *A Documentary History of Art*, ed. Elizabeth G. Holt (Princeton, New Jersey: Princeton University Press, 1982), vol. II, 980.

[30] *Lettres à Madame Hanska*, 4 vols. (Paris: Editions du Delta, 1967), I, 506.

[31] Gustave Flaubert, *Correspondance*, 13 vols. (Paris: Conard-Lambert, 1926-1954), I, 426.

[32] *A la recherche du temps perdu*, II, 327.

[33] Georges Rouault, *Sur l'art et sur la vie* (Paris: Denoël-Gonthier, 1971), p. 94.

[34] Roger Bordier, *L'Objet contre l'art* (Paris: Hachette, 1972), p. 94.

[35] Bordier, p. 93.

[36] Quoted in Dora Vallier, *Repères: La Peinture en France, début et fin d'un système visuel*, 1870-1970 (Paris: Alfieri et Lacroix, 1976), p. 79.

[37] George Sand, *Correspondance* IV, 711.

[38] Flaubert, *Correspondance* III, 8.

[39] Quoted in Daniel Wildenstein, *Monet*, 3 vols. (Lausanne: La Bibliothèque des Arts, 1974-1979), III, 650. Jean-Pierre Hoschédé, *Monet*, 2 vols. (Genève: Pierre Cailler, 1960), II, 109-110.

[40] Alain Robbe-Grillet, *Pour un nouveau roman* (Paris: Gallimard, collection Idées, 1963), p. 30.

[41] see Dora Vallier, *Repères*. Louis Goldaine, Pierre Astier *Ces peintres vous parlent* (Paris: L'Oeil du temps, 1964). Jean Grenier. *Entretiens avec dix-sept peintres non figuratifs* (Paris: Calmann-Lévy, 1963).

[42] André Lhote, *Les Invariants plastiques: Manet et Picasso* (Paris: Hermann, 1967), p. 83.

[43] Moreau is quoted by André Chastel, *L'Image dans le miroir* (Paris: Gallimard, collection Idées, 1980), p. 191.

[44] Quoted in Donald E. Gordon, "Ernst Ludwig Kirchner: By Instinct Possessed," *Art in America*, November 1980, pp. 81-95, see p. 90.

[45] Monroe Beardsley, *Aesthetics: Problems in the Philosophy of Criticism* (New York: Harcourt, Brace & World, Inc., 1958), p. 460.

[46] *Picasso's Mask*, trans. June Guicharnaud with Jacques Guicharnaud (New York: Holt, Rhinehart, Winston, 1974), p. 140.

[47] Quoted in Jean-Claude Lebensjtejn, "Les textes du peintre," *Critique*, no. 324, mai 1974, p. 425.

[48] Flaubert is quoted by Maupassant in the preface to *Pierre et Jean*.

[49] Paul Gauguin, *45 lettres à Vincent, Théo et Jo Van Gogh* (Lausanne: La Bibliothèque des Arts, 1983), p. 185.

[50] Paul Gauguin, *Letters to Ambroise Vollard and André Fontainas*, ed. John Rewald (San Francisco: The Grabhorn Press, 1943), p. 47.

[51] Gauguin, *Letters to Ambroise Vollard and André Fontainas*, p. 31.

[52] Ibid., p. 32.

[53] See Emile Bernard, "Souvenirs sur Paul Cézanne et lettres inédites," *Mercure de France*, 1 et 15 octobre 1907. See 1 octobre 1907, p. 400.

[54] Camille Pissarro, *Letters to his son Lucien*, ed. John Rewald with the assistance of Lucien Pissarro, 3rd ed. (Mamaroneck, New York: Paul Appel, 1972), p. 221.

[55] Emile Bernard, *Mercure de France*, 1 octobre 1907, p. 394-395.

Three novelists in search of their art: Gustave Flaubert,
Marcel Proust, Roger Martin du Gard

The novelists grouped in this chapter exemplify the self-doubt, uncertainty, anguish and dissatisfaction that many artists suffer. All were unsure that they had chosen the right path and often wondered if love of literature and a desire to write was justification enough to embark on a career as a novelist. None was ever sure he had talent, a subject, or the tenacity and moral courage required to be a writer. Even after publication of his work, each had doubts about its value and his accomplishment. All three wrote works unpublished in their lifetime,—in the case of Flaubert and Proust, juvenilia kept in drawers. Flaubert reworked one of his early manuscripts, *La Tentation de saint Antoine*, over a period of twenty eight years, producing three different versions of the novel. The final one appeared in 1874. His *L'Education sentimentale* (1869) grew out of a sketch composed in 1838 and a first draft written in 1843-1845. In *Remembrance of Things Past*, Proust, like Flaubert before him, used many themes present in his first unfinished novel, *Jean Santeuil*. He set it aside after working on it for four years. In the case of Martin du Gard, who destroyed all of his early writing, it is not possible to know precisely to what extent the themes of his mature work were already present in his juvenilia.

None of these men considered himself a born raconteur; story-telling was an art each had to learn. All three had difficulty with details, for example, often feeling that plot construction prevented them from channeling time and energy more effectively. Flaubert complained that, while writing *La Tentation de saint Antoine* (first version), he spent so much time on each pearl that he had forgotten the string holding them together.[1] The fear of being bogged down in detail was augmented by anxiety that less of it would make their novels lifeless and too abstract.

There are few artists whose creative process is as well documented as Flaubert's and yet, as Maurice Bardèche once noted,

we know very little about its genesis and development.[2]   There
are even fewer artists in whom we can see so clearly the factors
leading to perpetual self-doubt, self-imposed torture and constant dissatisfaction with and temptation to destroy one's work.
No writer was as distrustful of himself, of imagination, of inspiration, of anything that gave him satisfaction as an artist.   Flaubert felt the need to sacrifice all expression of his individuality,
of his personal points of view and of his beliefs, as if only in this
could he earn self-respect and the very partial certainty that he
had done the right thing.

He noted that impersonality is the sign of strength, that
the writer's art must serve only to help him feel what others feel
(*Corr.* III, 383-384).   The artist should eliminate any deforming
tendencies, be mirror-like in his accuracy of representation, and
become the "other" through total understanding.   Yet for Flaubert, writing was the expression of feelings—real, authentic and
sincere; if he didn't feel he was unable to write. Seeing the truth
objectively was not enough if it wasn't felt first (*Corr.* V, 385).
This insistence on feeling was coupled, as is well known, with a
belief that the impartiality of depiction must reach a point where
it has "the majesty of the law and the precision of science" (*Corr.*
V, 379).   As he himself stated, he worked from "contradictory
ideals" (*Corr.* VI, 2).   He wanted to feel no love, no pity and no
anger, and yet he couldn't forget his own reactions to what he
described (*Corr.* V, 397).   He aimed at impartiality and impersonality but put a lot of himself into everything he wrote: "I have
always put a lot of myself into everything I've done. In the place
of saint Antoine, I have put myself" (Corr. II, 461-462, also *Corr.*
I, 254).

Flaubert wanted to make us feel "materially" what he reproduced (Corr. II, 344-345), yet he wished to write a book about
nothing, where the subject would be almost invisible (Corr. II,
343-344).   He constantly stumbled against the inherent inadequacy of language, but style was for him the principal consideration in art.   He was interested primarily in truth but thought that
only the manner of seeing and depicting had any importance at
all: "There is no Truth!   There are only ways of seeing" (*Corr.*
VIII, 370).   If only the manner of depicting things had any importance, then originality was paramount, but it is difficult to reconcile this idea with the aims of objectivity and impersonality.
Flaubert claimed that what he felt most authentically and sincerely was what he could least express (*Corr.* III, 294), and yet express-

ivity and style of expression were of the utmost importance to
him. He believed that the artist needed great serenity and was
nauseated by the vulgarity and pettiness of most of what he
wrote about (*Corr.* III, 276). He was persuaded that an artist
doesn't choose his subject and yet he felt that the secret of producing masterpieces lies in the harmony ("concordance") between
the subject and the author's temperament (*Corr.* V, 466). But
how was he to reconcile this belief with his ideas on impersonality? Aware that he worked with "contradictory ideals," he added
that these caused a sense of blockage and impotence (*Corr.* VI, 2).
Such feelings of powerlessness are dangerous for any artist as
they are obviously a drain on his emotional energy; they raise
the fear that he has reached a dead end. Flaubert's powerlessness
appeared, to him, to delineate the boundary he would not be able
to cross, and it was as if he were a prisoner within it.

When Flaubert stated that he wrote things as he felt them
and therefore as he thought they existed, he accorded an enormous amount of importance to the question of the artist's sensibility (*Corr.* V, 385). The question for him was: how does an artist feel and what does he feel? There was no doubt in his mind
that the artist must, at the very least, give the illusion that he
had felt first hand what he wrote about. Flaubert believed that
in many ways knowledge gained from observation and from
experience inhibited the artist's sensibility and prevented him
from perceiving or often from feeling spontaneously and sincerely. What an artist knows frequently limits and deadens his perspicacity and sensitivity. Very often, he doesn't know how to un-
ravel the mysteries and subtleties of what he has felt, a problem
experienced by the narrator of *Remembrance of Things Past* as
well.

Flaubert knew that only sincere feeling is liberating and
stimulating, allowing one to capture diverse and often violently
new and unsettling things. Since limits are part of the human
lot, imagination must be, in some sense, the ability to go beyond
them. The artist is chronically dissatisfied with what his knowledge often imposes upon him, with what is taken for granted,
with what others consider usual, normal, moral or good. Flaubert asked: "Mustn't one, to be an artist, see everything in a different way than other men do?" (*Corr.* III, 33-34).

Proust's narrator makes the same point when he notes
that for each man the realm of reality is in his own sensibility
(III, 884). What the artist feels, when he is rid of the anesthetiz-

ing effect of his own prejudices, is a difficult questioʌ
wrote to a correspondent that Breughel's painting oʈ
name had inspired him to write *La Tentation de sain.*
 but his personal experience largely furnished him the ʟ
he drew on to write *Madame Bovary, L'Education se.*
tale," "Un coeur simple," and even parts of *Salammbô.* Pʟ ʟust's
narrator claims that everything he will recount was inspired by
the experience of the cup of tea and the madeleine. Henry James
wrote to his brother that he did not use real persons as models
but had to rely for his creations on his "moral consciousness"
(*Notebooks*, 67).

The statements by Proust's narrator and by Henry James
indicate that the creation of characters is not always primarily
based on the observation of people or on the imitation of "real
life" models. As James implies, observation strengthens the impressions which arise and develop in the artist's moral consciousness. The observation of individual persons is not the
first or even most basic element. Flaubert wrote that it was necessary for him to create a model in his imagination and have it
"pose" for him in his mind (*Corr.* III, 269). He was not speaking
of a model copied from life. His view of the role of the imagination is at variance with one held by Boris Pasternak who said of
his contemporary Andrei Beily:

> His scope is comparable to that of chamber music—never greater. If
> he had really suffered he might have written the major work of
> which he was capable. But he never came into contact with real
> life.[3]

It is almost as if Pasternak equated real life with suffering; he
also implied that precisely because Beily never felt anything deeply he never came into contact with real life.

Flaubert knew very well that he could not create any characters if he did not put himself into their flesh. But in a sense he
was already his creations. He had put so much of himself into
his characters that he had modeled them in his own image. The
writer could become the character he created only if he understood him (or her) completely and felt as he or she did. In order
to carry this off successfully, he was forced to rely on observation
of others but even more, on what he had observed of himself
and of his feelings. When he undertook to write the story of
Madame Delamare as a *pensum* to rid himself of the excesses of
passion and lyricism, he thought that he assumed the personal-

ity and some of the limitations of the heroine who became Madame Bovary.

It is noteworthy that many of Flaubert's contemporaries had quite another approach to the same problem. George Sand, for instance, wrote to Balzac in 1839 that her characters were three quarters pure invention as she felt she neither could nor would copy a living model. Flaubert aimed at reaching a point where he could no longer distinguish between what the model had given him and what he had added of his own invention or of himself; when the contours of the real and the imagined blended perfectly, he knew he had arrived at what he wanted (*Corr. Supp.* I, 226; *Corr.* IV, 61). Although the artist's feelings were for Flaubert the cornerstone of any work, he felt that personal feelings and reactions must disappear from the work in the sense that they should be expressed only by the characters. He noted that impersonality is the source of strength (*Corr.* II, 383-384). As for imagination, he decried its "falsehood" and "nonsense" (*Corr.* III, 105).

Imagination thus produces only subjective, irrational, uncontrollable and insubstantial visions. The criticism to which Bouilhet and Ducamp subjected the first version of *La Tentation de saint Antoine* most likely reinforced Flaubert's reasons for distrusting imagination in general and his own in particular. Flaubert's misgivings concerning the imagination, echoed in 1874 by the art critic Castagnary, were in fact a commonplace of criticism at the time:

> The case of M. Cézanne (*A Modern Olympia*) can serve as a warning of the fate in store for the Impressionists. They will go from one idealization to another, until they reach such a pitch of unrestrained romanticism that Nature is no more than a pretext for dreaming and the imagination becomes incapable of formulating anything except personal and subjective fantasies, without a trace of general rationality, because they are uncontrolled and cannot possibly be verified in reality.[4]

What Castagnary most probably didn't know was that Cézanne was more distrustful of imagination than any artist of his time and was quoted as saying: "I fear nothing as much as imagination."[5] Joachim Gasquet quoted the painter as saying that his only method was the hatred of the imaginative.[6] No doubt Cézanne hated imagination precisely for the reasons stated by Castagnary, which were the same ones that had inspired Flaubert's reservations and those of his friends. In many ways, Flaubert's attitude toward his work reminds us of that of his contemporaries, the Impressionists, who painted not only the subject itself but their reactions to it, believing that in these reactions imagination showed itself in its proper form. Like them, Flaubert felt that art is not a replication of reality, but rather the expression of feelings stimulated by reality, outer and inner.

Monet said that the subject was something of no significance for him, that he wanted to reproduce what was between the subject and himself. His work was to be the expression of what he personally had felt, and a similar remark was made by Cézanne. As Castagnary had predicted in 1874, insistence on pure expression of personal feelings prefigures the total disappearance of the concept and the model in art. But Flaubert was afraid to go as far as Monet, who sounds, at times, in the above remarks, like an expressionist. Cézanne, like Flaubert, felt the need to use external reality as a basis for art but he was afraid of what he called the changeability and instability of nature. It is precisely to hold a fleeting, unstable reality that he sought to make of Impressionism "something solid and durable like the art in museums."[7] Cézanne seemed reluctant to think that purely personal reactions to the subject were the most important consideration since such reactions were also often based on something insubstantial and evanescent.

If Flaubert distrusted the purely imaginary element it was because he too feared that it did not have the solidity, the weight, and the breadth of reality. He attempted to blend imagination and observation to create an art that would seem valid to him. He claimed that artistic observation must be instinctive and proceed from the imagination but also that it must be strengthened by the use of what he called "secours étrangers" or exterior elements (*Corr.* III, 230). His use of these words indicates that for him such elements were the equivalent of what T. S. Eliot would later call objective correlatives. Most artists need such correlatives although many graphic artists in the twentieth century have felt that if a correlative is needed, it too should be imagined or invented. For them, the artist's task is to imagine a correlative which then serves him to express his feelings.

Flaubert still believed in the necessity of exterior elements to support the weight of the imaginary construct, whereas Proust, who needed them just as much, wrote that reality just didn't hold up. He believed that the artist uses elements taken from reality, but that these must be reworked and transformed if they are to be of any help to him. Many artists need an objective correlative because they feel that imagination is insufficient if they themselves do not experience, at least in thought, what they have imagined. Flaubert wrote, probably somewhat ironically, that Emma Bovary could only understand what she had experienced. Most artists would agree that this statement applies to them as well. No less a poet than Keats stated: "Nothing ever becomes real until it is experienced" (letter of 19 March, 1819). If the artist is not to be imprisoned in his subjectivity, he must feel what others have felt. Keats noted: "I feel more and more as my imagination strengthens, that I do not live in this world alone but in a thousand worlds" (letter of October 24, 1818).

In the same way, Flaubert believed that through empathy and sympathy he had reached a point where he could say he had been "a boatman on the Nile . . . a Greek rhetorician in Suburra . . . a pirate and monk, tumbler and coachman . . . (*Corr.* V, 240). The transformative power of imagination and sympathy enabled him to feel what another being experiences to the point of exchanging identities, but this left him thinking that the self, personal experience and emotion form an unstable core. He remarked that his self "scattered" in books to such an extent that he spent whole days "without feelings of self-consciousness" (*Corr.* VI, 441). Thus he seemed to be on a merry-go-round chasing the self which was fragmented and dispersed throughout all his works. He was left feeling that he had transferred so much of himself to his characters that there was little left of his own identity. The creation had almost exhausted the creator. But this was not an entirely unwanted phenomenon as he had written that he was so disgusted with life that "in order not to live, I plunged into Art, like a desperate man" (Corr. IV, 356).

Convinced as he was that we can only know what we have felt, Flaubert strangely enough had very little to say on the question of how the artist can understand the thoughts and sensibilities of others so as to grasp reality as *they* experience it. He knew this was neither easy nor "natural" and wrote that he had difficulty in making himself feel (*Corr.* III, 97). The psychiatrist R. D. Laing recently wrote that we are "totally incapable of knowing what happens out of the boundaries of our own experience. And even there . . . "[8] The novelist Lawrence Durrell once stated during an interview that readers do not clearly understand how limited an experience of life most artists have.[9] Evidently, they hope to compensate through feelings of sympathy for their lack of experience and for the difficulty they have in penetrating into the mind of a character. Generally, artists have had little to say on how they succeeded in reaching the needed state of empathy. Many have not known if they were describing what a character felt or if they were projecting their own feelings onto their creations. But artists who do create authentic characters may then face the problem Conrad complained of: "What bothers me most is that my characters are so true. I know them so well that they shackle the imagination."[10]

Flaubert was fully conscious of the difficulty of feeling what another feels, of "transforming oneself into the character" (*Corr.* V, 257). It was his greatest wish to feel he had become another being, "even if only for three seconds" (*Corr.* IV, 212), as this is the closest one can come to the sensation of understanding another. He never discussed his reasons for wanting to identify with another being. Did he believe characters are other possible versions of oneself, "des possibles," as Gide later said? Could such identification bring greater self-knowledge? Did it help one to escape the anguish of solipsism? Did it perhaps enable the writer to have the consciousness of another, thus leading to greater knowledge of the world? Was it a way of transcending the limitations Flaubert hated? (*Corr.* II, 366).

From various passages in his correspondence, one can guess that as Flaubert understood it, the novelists's task is mainly to get at the truth. This justified for him the creation of believable, lifelike characters and descriptions. They in turn were the guarantors of the truth presented by the artist. If the novelist failed and created unbelievable characters or situations, he could not communicate any sense of the exactness of what he felt or imagined. If Flaubert's novels were based on a belief in verisimilitude, it was because this quality was needed to convince the reader and support the weight of the author's imaginative creations. The Impressionist painters had abandoned verisimilitude or at least insisted on stressing their feelings and their personal reactions to what they saw. Flaubert still thought of himself as an objective artist, whose task it was to define, analyze and understand. The stress was somewhat different because his temperament pulled him in the direction of expressivity and his esthetic in another, that of verisimilitude.

The belief in the necessity and importance of verisimilitude lasted much longer among writers than among painters.

The idea that the writer can and must create other beings and identify with them in order to gain insights he transmits to his readers is one which survived unshaken until it was questioned by the Surrealists. One of the first persons to attack it was André Breton, who stated that imagination has every power except that of enabling one to identify with other people.[11] Flaubert's statement on the difficulty of making himself feel things in general, and more particularly those experienced by his characters, indicates his doubts as to the powers his contemporaries so readily attributed to the imagination. He also made several statements showing another side of his experience and these illustrate his manner of working. He spoke of his ability to stir up feelings in himself when he held a pen in his hand and noted that he was a "man-pen" and that he felt emotions through the pen and because of it (*Corr. I*, 362; *Corr. II*, 72, 364; *Corr. III*, 97). Flaubert had become the instrument of his craft and saw his function, his aim in life, as that of a writer exclusively.

If at times he found it difficult to sympathize with his characters or to experience what he had described, at other times he had only to begin writing to be swept along by empathy. By the physical act of writing he surmounted the problem of identifying with characters or moods. His statements on the capacity for emotion that writing brought him, and on the emotion itself, make it clear that working gave him a natural, spontaneous way to feel and understand his subject; it led him in the right direction toward truth. All he had to do was let himself be carried by the rhythm of his writing. It appears that he did not have to impose much control on himself as long as his critical conscience did not intervene.

His statement about "this faculty for emotion that writing gives me without my having anything to do with it, and which comes in spite of myself, in an often embarrassing manner" indicates that usually he had to reimpose restrictions and control upon his work because what he wrote brought an almost uncontrollable emotion (*Corr. II*, 72). He had to struggle to restrain himself, and often had to change what he had produced under the influence of the emotion which had come to him, in spite of himself, while he wrote. The conscious artist had to rewrite those passages produced by a more free-flowing, undirected or uncontrolled emotion, itself brought about by spontaneous writing.

At other times, however, he complained that he had to

force himself to feel anything (*Corr.* III, 156). He also complained that he constantly had to get into the skin of people whom he did not like, who were unlikeable ("antipathiques") (*Corr.* III, 146). He realized that even if he felt something he attributed to one of his characters, he would have to re-experience the feeling, but artificially to be sure, in order to set it down (*Corr.* III, 146). Writing of past feelings must be done coldly. When he was not under their direct impression, the intensity of the feelings and the way they were experienced had to be recreated, reconstituted from memory, a task all artists face at one time or another.

Flaubert seemed ill at ease when he dealt with characters from antiquity. In one of his letters he asked rhetorically, with references to such figures as Salammbô, Saint Antoine and Hérodias, if anyone had ever seen the model, the type upon which these characters are based (*Corr.* IV, 330). But he knew he could not create characters based solely on models from antiquity for such works as *Salammbô*, or "Hérodias;" a character is always a composite. He noted that with his reconstruction of the civilization of Carthage he had undertaken too difficult a task. This did not prevent him for piecing together a Carthage made up of imagined elements blended with what he had gathered from historical sources, and even from events of his own time.

The resulting montage did in fact impress him as being based on a complex but interesting reality. What the artist reproduces was for Flaubert an amalgam of elements blended in very diverse and indeterminable proportions. He noted that he had imagined, remembered and combined these elements (*Corr.* I, 254). Although he knew that the artist must imagine, remember and combine everything, Flaubert also believed that by giving free rein to his imagination the writer encompasses the greatest scope. If a writer restricts himself to facts, he limits his work to the contingent and relative. Flaubert's inclination was to let himself be carried away by his imaginative power, but he was afraid of this power and distrusted it. He was torn between "the sonority of prose, lyricism, the great flights of eagles, all the sonorities of the sentence and the summits of ideas," and a desire to make readers feel what he wrote about "in its very materiality" (*Corr.* II, 343-344, January 16, 1852).

He found combining material and non-material elements very difficult. He noted, for example: "One must, by an effort of the mind, transport oneself into the characters and not pull them toward oneself" (*Corr.* V, 257). He had remarked earlier that he thought he was wrong not to abandon himself to his inclination for "lyricism, violence, excentricities" as that would at least make him write a work that was really his (*Corr.* II, 322). Whereas "abandoning" oneself indicates an effortless letting go and yielding to one's natural instinct, understanding others by experiencing what they have felt is an arduous if not impossible task. One must go out of oneself, "transport oneself into the characters" and refuse to be swept off by inner impulses.

When he spoke of a work that would be his, Flaubert showed that there was a difference between following the inclination of one's inner self and crossing terrain not one's own. He wondered if he had merely transferred his own feelings to his characters. He was fully conscious of having always put himself into everything he wrote (*Corr.* II, 461).

These words contain a self-reproach and an expression of doubt concerning his success in creating autonomous, independent characters. The difficulties of escaping one's self loomed before him. He feared that in his attempts to become another he had failed doubly. He had not been able to be the other and by attempting to do so had lost or diminished his own selfhood. For him imagination consisted largely in answering the question of what it is to feel as another being does, and how this is done. Can the artist become the other by sheer force of will, or must he be passive and wait for it to happen? A writer can ask himself how he would react in the circumstances faced by his characters, but this too might amount simply to putting himself into everything he does. According to Flaubert, "Everything lies in this: to draw from oneself" (*Corr.* II, 409). There is no other possibility than using one's own personal, limited experience. This must be done in spite of the danger of not being able to go beyond oneself.

The problems encountered by Flaubert daunted him continually, and he claimed to feel ever more acutely his failings and limitations. He noted once that he lacked the energy to do away with himself—a drastic solution—but the only one which would end his torment, as he couldn't give up writing while he remained alive (*Corr.* VII, 5). His sense of powerlessness can be seen clearly in the many remarks he made concerning language and the numerous problems he had with it, the principal one being that he was torn between contradictory notions on the subject. He professed admiration for and agreement with La Bruyère's maxim that the main task of the artist is to define accurately and to depict clearly. He spent a great deal of time convincing himself that he should try to describe reality very faithfully, as if the accuracy of the representation insured its truth. But he soon came to the conclusion that the search for words was impossibly difficult and that to try to describe what he imagined was fruitless since there were no words for such things. Echoing his creator, one of Flaubert's protagonists asks how it is possible to even think one can render the "impressions of the heart, these mysteries of the soul unknown to itself."[12]

Flaubert felt that language was not precise, rich, subtle, flexible, or adaptable enough for the artist's purposes. There was no solid link between words and thoughts or feeling. The gap between words and their referent was too wide, in fact unbridgeable. Language distorts thoughts and emotions, making communication impossible. Similar points had already been made numerous times, and Wittgenstein, for example, was to write that language disguises thought. Werner Hoffman, who quotes the philosopher's remarks in his article "Marcel Duchamp and Emblematic Realism," states that Duchamp gave up art precisely because he thought it was impossible to use language to transcribe the artist's intention or the substance and quality of his imagined or conceptual reality.[13]   Flaubert felt exactly the same way: "I succeed in expressing the one hundredth part of my ideas after endless groping" (*Corr.* V, 252-253). He believed that he felt most sincerely what he expressed most badly and remarked that the less one felt something, the easier it was to express it accurately (*Corr.* II, 294, 462). He thought that he himself was born with a "special" language whose key he alone possessed (*Corr.* I, 239). He had to learn to communicate this personal language in his art and to create the means of making it accessible to others, or be imprisoned in solipsism.

As to the ordinary difficulties writers encounter every day of their working lives, Flaubert wavered. Sometimes he felt that simple natural expression doesn't come without effort, but that it is nevertheless possible to find it. If so, there would be an accordance between language and the artist's idea. At other times, he felt the futility of trying to achieve agreement between what he wanted and the means he had available, and complained that plasticity of style was not sufficient for his ideas. He added that this was a fault inherent in language and that there were too many things to express and not enough ways to do so (*Corr.* III, 157).

Flaubert believed language to be unsuited to the artist's needs and neither transparent nor pliable enough. Far from being transparent, it calls attention to itself and distracts both writer and reader from its function of representation and communication. It is loaded down with cultural and intellectual biases which are obstacles to the artist who must use it in a special manner. If Flaubert believed that he was born with a special language whose key he alone possessed, and that he couldn't communicate with those who did not understand this language, he also knew that he had to translate his language into the intrinsically inadequate one already in existence. While working on *Salammbô* he wrote that the insufficiency of vocabulary was such that very often he was forced to change details of his story. Exactitude was impossible; truth was inaccessible (*Corr.* V, 287). The artist, according to Flaubert, is forced to simplify or alter the truth. He is obliged to invent and teach his readers a new language, one in which they do not normally think (*Corr.* IV, 279). Only in this way can he hope to overcome the gaps between imagination and language, and between imagination and reality. Language was of such importance to Flaubert because he believed that style was the "lifeblood of thought" (*Corr.* III, 336). This statement implies that the writer is the discover of truth, the giver of meaning, and that it is through the originality of his work that meaning and value are created. Without him the world is a lifeless backdrop, devoid of significance. It can only acquire significance when transformed by the artist.

The idea that style is the lifeblood of thought implies that reality is not a yardstick for the artist. There is no outside model to which he must conform. Each artist creates his own model and does not always need to resort to reality to measure the truth, coherence or comprehensiveness of his creation. Flaubert claimed that there is a gap between the knower and the known, between the author and what he says, between what is said and how it is said. But sometimes the gap can be closed. It is interesting that the novelist Romain Gary (1914-1981) felt that he had reached a state of perfect agreement between what he wanted to do and what he had accomplished, and saw no reason to continue living. This is the reason he himself gave for his suicide, which he did not want to be misunderstood. The explanation of his suicide was, according to him, to be found in the last line of his last novel: "I have finally expressed myself completely."[14]

Language had an overwhelming importance for Flaubert

because he believed that "the idea exists only through its form" (*Corr.* I, 321). This statement implies that only that which has a form can exist. If language cannot give ideas a form, then ideas cannot exist. The artist is a real creator because he gives form to what did not have any before. Since language is inadequate, the artist's work will be inadequate as well unless he can create a language of his own, one unique to himself. Valéry echoed this when he noted: "My idea was to create an artificial language based on the reality of thought" (*Cahiers* XIII, 280).

Even if a writer creates a language of his own, he may still be betrayed by it. Language is dangerous because it petrifies thought. It can also defeat a writer's purpose because he cannot control it. This is because "Style is as much under words as in words" (*Corr.* IV, 315). This statement can mean that connotation is as important as denotation, or that what artists imply is as important as what they write, or that the reader has an essential role to play as he construes the implications of a work, or that the reader must judge whether what is implied contradicts the words implying it. He may also have to decide if a work contains one meaning deducible from what is not explicitly stated but can be inferred.

The reader, then, infers meaning from what is "under the words" or from a "tension" between statements. He ultimately decides whether any meanings are to be inferred, what they are, and why they are most important. It may be up to him to decide if an artist has written two works in one. The problem described by Flaubert and others of dealing with a language inadequate to the artist's vision is summarized neatly in Valéry's *Cahiers*: "Literature tries to create through words the state of the lack of words" (XVIII, 350). It is from within the very inadequacy of his medium that any artist must work to overcome that inadequacy.

For this reason the painter Gustave Moreau noted that the colors he saw around him were totally useless to him and that a painter must imagine the colors used to transcribe his inner vision. When he wrote *Salammbô* Flaubert remarked that he had to invent a language people did not think in so as to compensate for the inadequacy of ordinary language and to present a world long vanished and forgotten (*Corr.* IV, 279). Of *Madame Bovary*, he noted that he had written only a "true and almost literal account of what must have happened" (*Corr.* IV, 61).

For Keats a synthesis such as Flaubert attempted was not of primary importance. He appears not to have valued the work itself and wrote: ". . . every mental pursuit takes its reality and worth from the pursuer—being in itself a nothing—ethereal thing . . ." (Letter of 13 March 1818). For him it was only the emotional charge with which artists invest their work that had value or meaning. Wordsworth also spoke of the necessity of "infusing by meditation into the objects with which it [the mind] converses an intellectual life" (*The Friend*, January 4, 1810). These thoughts show both poets' conviction that it is from the intensity and sincerity of the artist's emotional charge that any artistic endeavor has value. The creator's aim is not always primarily to fashion a work of beauty nor to communicate to and share with others a special vision. The novelist and critic Bernard Pingaud, for instance, wrote that once the work is completed it often closes in upon itself and excludes the artist completely.[15] Flaubert, with his emphasis on impersonality, was not very far from the very same belief that the work excludes its author and is self-reflexive. He also stated: "Art is great because it makes us better" (*Corr.* I, 428). Art challenges the artist to develop, to fulfill his potential, to go beyond his limits, and the fact that he may produce a great work is secondary as is the question of what he has expressed of himself in that work.

In spite of the life-long torment Flaubert went through in the creation of his work and despite his feelings of artistic impotence, self-doubt, and fear of not having done the best he was capable of, he never destroyed anything he wrote. Yet he said that he saw more clearly every day the nullity of what he thought was his best effort (*Corr.* II, 48-49). The reason Flaubert never destroyed his work was that however dissatisfied he was with it, he never felt he had reached the limit of his possibilities, a point from which he could go no further. As he never thought he had reached such a barrier, he was not humiliated in his own eyes by feelings of failure and unworthiness. This possibility of maintaining his self-respect, his sense of having accomplished something which demanded the best effort he could give, was a source of strength to him. The idea of discovering his capabilities challenged him (*Corr.* II, 364). He had, of course, many moments of "inner humiliation" when things did not go well, when he was disappointed and discouraged with the results of his efforts (*Corr.* II, 383).

The fact that Flaubert did not know how far he could go prompted him to keep writing until he knew what "the power of his muscles" was (*Corr.* II, 364). He was also extremely fortunate in having the support of his friend Louis Bouilhet, whose judgment he trusted fully, for better or for worse. The eminent critic Gérard Genette has written that Flaubert, protesting all the while, nevertheless accepted Bouilhet's criticism submissively and did not reject his "castrating" influence.[16]   Bouilhet would not have given any advice if Flaubert had not specifically and repeatedly asked for it.   By trusting his friend to the extent that he did, Flaubert probably and quite unconsciously delegated to him decisions he himself did not want to make.   He permitted his friend to have a voice in the revisions of his manuscripts and undoubtedly may have given him more latitude than was desirable. This disadvantage was more than offset by the support he received from one of the very few persons whose advice and encouragement he respected and accepted.   The support of his friend was invaluable when Flaubert was tried for outrage to public morals upon the publication of *Madame Bovary*, and when *Salammbô* was poorly received in 1862.   When Bouilhet died in July 1869, Flaubert lamented the disappearance of the "midwife" of his thought.   He saw no point in continuing his work as he had lost the one person for whom it was intended (*Corr.* VI, 102, 115, 121, 451).

Flaubert's lack of confidence was due in great part to his belief that he was not an original writer.   He noted that everything had already been said, and said so well that he couldn't add much (*Corr.* I, 426; *Corr.* II, 329).   But he also remarked that he had new things to contribute by virtue of his being of his era (*Corr.* III, 137); it seemed to him that he alone felt certain things, as yet unsaid, that only he could express (*Corr.* II, 363).   But in a letter to Bouilhet he deplored the inhibiting nature of his artistic self-consciousness, his excessive scruples, his preoccupation with good taste.   Most original artists are by temperament less self-conscious than he was, less concerned with theory and technical problems, less inclined to doubt their talent and to see difficulties everywhere.   They have a boldness ("audace"), a spontaneity, a sense of freedom and purpose he could never attain (*Corr.* II, 235).

He never defined originality.   Yet for him this word contained a contradiction.   He believed that one part of it was the individuality of the creative person.   Some had only to shriek to be harmonious, to cry to move others, and to take themselves as their subject to be universal.   But the real masters never think of themselves or their passions and are still able to encompass humanity. He knew he was not of the caliber of Montaigne and Byron who created works of art simply by expressing their thoughts and feelings. Nor, of course, did he consider himself one of the "real masters" (*Corr.* II, 385). He did not believe that he could boast any worthwhile individuality. Even if he could, he did not want to trade on it in his art. He considered individuality a secondary virtue. He thought he had a chance of contributing something if he created works distinguished by their precision, understatement and craftsmanship. But as is well known, he could not forget his individuality. He regretted his inability to abandon himself to his bent for lyricism, violence and lyrico-fantastic "excentricities" as they would probably inspire him to write a work that was really his (*Corr.* II, 322).

If Flaubert had no faith in his originality, it was also because he refused to believe in the possibility of any creative endeavor in his own age. He said that nineteenth-century artists had great technical knowledge and resources but no solid grounding, or "intrinsic principle;" they lacked the "soul, the idea of art" (*Corr.* II, 202). In view of this, originality was unthinkable. He contrasted his time with the Old Regime and stated that the earth trembled under him. He was conscious of living after an upheaval. Society had changed so completely that it was now necessary for the artist to reinvent art itself before creating his work. A similar idea was to occur to Proust's narrator who complained that the great works of the nineteenth century were all unfinished, apparently because a solid justification for them was lacking. To remedy this lack, nineteenth-century artists drew their working principle from an awareness of their creative processes (III, 160-161).

Like Balzac, who was haunted by the subject, Flaubert feared the drying up of his vital energies. He said that writing a novel was like moving mountains, draining him both physically and mentally (*Corr.* II, 384). This remark shows that artists often wonder if once creative energy is used up, they will be able to find any more within themselves; they seem to believe it is a nonrenewable resource and become anxious about channeling and using it effectively. Flaubert claimed from the very beginning that as time passed he became more timid (*Corr.* IV, 178; V, 159), fearful (*Corr.* V. 225), sterile (*Corr.* II, 210), less intelligent (*Corr.* II, 169), more exacting in his demands upon himself (*Corr.* I, 203). He felt his imagination slowly declining (*Corr.* I, 233, 255; IV, 336; *Supp.* I, 270). Five years before his death he complained

that he was losing his faith in himself (*Supp.* I, 270). No worse
fate could have befallen him, since he felt that belief in himself
was his only possible support (*Corr.* I, 53).

****

It is clear from the *Carnet 1908*, as well as from his correspondence, that Proust, like Flaubert, had to surmount what he
considered serious obstacles before he could become a writer. He
did not know whether his work would be a novel, an essay or a
philosophical study and he wondered if he was really a novelist.[17] He noted that laziness, self-doubt, and feelings of artistic
impotence entered into his indecision about the form his work
would assume (*C 1908*, 61). Only his fear of death and his conviction that he could make an original contribution eventually,
helped him to overcome his self-doubts (*C 108*, 60-61). Proust's
belief that he had something unique to transmit was one that he
shared with many other artists. For such artists, this is usually
the decisive factor in conquering all inner obstacles. Proust's
sense of a mission, and his fear of squandering his special gift,
was shared, for instance, by Wordsworth, Flaubert and Gauguin.

Proust's illness was a major factor in his effort to finally
get down to work and stop wasting time; he wrote about himself:
"Soon you will not be able to say all this" in fear that death
would not wait for him to finish if he procrastinated (*C 1908*, 61.
He also reproached himself for entertaining a "meaning" for so
long without doing any writing that he had forgotten his original inspiration and allowed the creative emotion to dry up (*C
1908*, p. 69). This was a serious reproach and he noted later that
intelligence and reason do not create but can only arrange, order
or clarify. Real creation for an artist means going more deeply
into reminiscences, as these are the stuff of which his inner
sense of his work is made (*C 1908*, p. 101). Proust had been
carrying this conception within him but had not yet successfully
given form to it.

These self-reproaches jotted down in the 1908 diary are a
summary of those the narrator of *Remembrance of Things Past*
would later level against himself. In becoming a novelist,
Proust experienced many of the same problems as his narrator.
The story of the latter's efforts to write the book he has dreamed

of since childhood is, or course, one of the subjects of *Remembrance of Things Past*. For most of his life, the narrator cannot understand or recreate experiences that have been repressed and forgotten in the depths of his subconscious. He cannot believe that he has any original insights, or even admit the possibility that he might have anything new to say. He cannot escape the deadening effect of habit, the danger of believing that art must have an "intellectual" value and the custom of registering unimportant exterior reality. He is too lazy to study, analyze, and shape the only significant reality,—the innermost self. Other perplexities faced by Proust and his narrator include a belief in solipsism, the inability to understand one's constantly changing personality, and the difficulty of understanding others and communicating with them.

The narrator appears to himself as a being whose perceptions and impressions are all inspired by and indebted to the creations of other artists. But this is true of everyone. The narrator notes that original works have a beauty people cannot see because it is obscured by our habit of seeing in a certain way; in other words, we do not really look at things at all (III, 722). We do not see them in the way they should be seen—without preconceptions about what we like or know. Every original artist destroys the spell under which his predecessors hold the public.

The narrator explains that another obstacle he faces is a tendency to draw abstractions and generalizations from reality to such an extent that it becomes invisible and hence incomprehensible. When he goes to a dinner party, he does not see the guests because he is too busy x-raying them; viewed this way their individuality is lost because their flesh and blood disappear (III, 719). Roger Martin du Gard had similar problems, believing that he loaded his work with so many theories—mainly psychological and social explanations of laws—as to overshadow the concrete life of his characters. Proust's narrator finally realizes that reality is only of limited use to the artist who cannot copy it but must create a world more meaningful and ordered than the one around him. But in doing so, he must not forget that his creation is based on a concrete reality which readers must recognize. Proust wrote in 1913 that reality disappoints and cannot equal our dreams. Yet the artist must take it as his point of departure, compensate for what it lacks, and give it the significance it otherwise does not have.

The artist's fear of being locked within himself is all the

greater when he feels his sensitivity to be dulled. He must put himself into the skin of another human being if he is to understand his fellow men. He must explain what he has experienced in such a way that his readers can understand him as well as themselves and others. This idea has been repeated throughout the ages. Wordsworth expressed it in the Preface to the *Lyrical Ballads,* and in the *Defence of Poetry* Shelley stated that the writer

> must put himself in the place of another and many others; the pains and pleasures of his species must become his own. The real instrument of the moral good is the imagination.

It seems that for Shelley, imagination is the ability to sympathize with others to such an extent that he is able to feel exactly as they do and to transport himself into another's soul to the point where he becomes that other person. Proust's narrator doubts that this imaginative inclination or effort can succeed. He believes that the only way of knowing oneself, or of knowing another, is through suffering, or through the emotional impact that the work of a great artist has on our sensibility. What our self-esteem, passion, imitative instinct, abstract intelligence and habit have constructed, art must undo (III, 896). While the narrator knows that only the accumulated experience of a lifetime could be the subject of his work, this lifetime experience overwhelms him (III, 1041-1042). In the second version of the Guermantes party episode, the narrator states that he doesn't know if he can keep before him the density of time past. It is not in the category of time that we see ourselves, he noted: "Otherwise we would see ourselves prolonged by all the invisible days that we have lived."[18]

Precisely because the past disappears, it is most difficult to bring it back to life. In the first version of the Guermantes party episode, the narrator calls time a sorcerer who metamorphoses things and persons so completely that they may be transformed out of all recognition, impossible to retrieve at all in their earlier forms. The narrator's sense of impotence in the face of such facts increases as a result of what he saw at the party. He wonders at that point if he will ever have the physical and emotional strength to write the work for which he now has a "subject" (III, 899). In the first version of the Guermantes party, the narrator deplores the fact that because of his age and illness, he no longer has "the obscure vitality of memory and of the creative instinct."[19] This sentence exactly resembles one written by Proust in the *Cahier 1908*. He notes there that for too long, he carried the "meaning" of things within himself and has forgotten much of it, his heart having meanwhile gone cold (p. 69).

At the same time that he finally gains enough confidence in himself to undertake the work he envisions, the narrator comes upon a scene of the decrepitude that time has wrought in the physical and mental condition of every person present at the Guermantes party. He worries that the intensity of the effort that will be needed to "resuscitate" the past and to find the words to express what he once felt might lead him to the brink of amnesia and aphasia. These are the words used by the narrator in the first version of the Guermantes party.[20] The tone is much more confident in the final version. There the narrator is certain that his efforts will be worthwhile because only through art can the "qualitative difference" in each individual's way of seeing the world be made understandable to others. If there were no art, each individual would be locked in an inner prison from which there would be no escape (III, 895).

The narrator eventually realizes that exterior reality inevitably disappoints the artist. This realization is for the best, as he is then forced to look much deeper within himself for the substance and meaning of his impressions. In Elstir's studio the narrator sees a watercolor which he finds enchanting, and attributes its charm to its subject. He originally believes that this charm had only to be discovered, observed and reproduced by the painter as it existed in nature (I, 847). But he soon realizes that this view of what a painter does is completely wrong. Later, the narrator understands that during his life Elstir had attempted to give form to an ideal which was the innermost part of himself (I, 851).

One day the painter meets an ideal form incarnate in the body of a woman, who becomes his wife. The result is that Elstir is able to paint from an exterior model instead of having to extract, at great pain, something deep within himself (I, 851). Having at the time reached an age when one no longer expects to realize one's ideal through the power of one's thought, Elstir needs the physical "satisfaction" of a living model to stimulate his tired mind. Proust implies that a decrease in creative power leads to materialism and to the likelihood of influences received passively (I, 851). Elstir thinks he can continue to work because

he has found his ideal realized in a model existing outside himself. When the period of the artist's strength is past, he turns to
his imitative skill and relies on it as well as on the inner intuition he found most propitious in the past. But he is then no
longer a great artist; he is not capable of the intellectual effort
which alone can produce a great work (I, 850-852).

Proust had noted on the last page of *Contre Sainte-Beuve*
(written in 1909, published in 1954) that there comes a time
when talent, like memory, weakens. Like Balzac and Flaubert,
Proust was quite conscious of the fact that an artist's powers
diminish with time. (Balzac believed it was intellectual effort itself which consumed an artist's vital energy). When he can no
longer make the intellectual effort necessary to tap what lies hidden in the depths of the inner self, the artist relies on the contem-
plation of exterior models and produces nothing more of real
value. But the narrator does not completely condemn Elstir. He
explains that some artists, even at the peak of their power, do
not have the "detachment" required to contemplate their inner
ideal and draw emotion from it (I, 850). Their ideal does not
appear clearly to them because they can only consider worthwhile and "divine" what is not themselves (I, 850). The narrator
implies that any artist with a clear conception of his ideal and its
true worth would be a self-idolator or narcissist. He indicates,
especially at the end of the novel, that a real artist cannot be a
narcissist. His only worth derives from the fact that he helps
others to understand themselves better, to know things they
would not otherwise have imagined.

As for Bergotte, long before he sees the Vermeer exhibit
and realizes that his own work pales in comparison, he has
already sensed that he no longer has any talent (I, 556). When he
reaches this conclusion, instead of tearing up what he had written, he tells himself that it is accurate and useful to his country
(I, 556). In his case as well, the narrator notes the necessity of
stimulating a spiritual machine which has become immobile
(III, 183). Bergotte tries to rekindle the flame of his dwindling
talent by loving a number of young girls (III, 183), but in the last
twenty years of his life writes nothing at all (III, 185).

Only the composer Vinteuil is apparently exempt from
the law of talent diminishing with age. The narrator sees that
the general public is correct in judging his last works to be his
greatest ones (III, 257). His last work, the *Septet*, is superior by far
to everything he has done before. Parts of the *Sonata* so beloved

by Swann appear, by contrast, totally banal to the point that one can't understand why it aroused so much admiration (III, 263). The composer's work is described as a "grimoire" or sorcerer's book of "undecipherable hieroglyphics" (III, 261). His daughter's friend spends years deciphering his papers and has "to guess at his orchestra indications" (III, 261). (Proust uses the word "deviner" and his English translators used the verb "interpret").

The composer's last years are darkened by the scandal of his daughter's misconduct. It nearly drives him mad, and hastens his death. She and her friend, the same lady who later "deciphers" his notes, are the laughing stock of Combray whose inhabitants reprove their lesbian relationship. Vinteuil does no creative work in his last years because he is unhappy and distraught by his daughter's behavior (I, 159-160). His anguish makes him abandon his plan of writing up all his notes. Most of his pieces he had not even jotted down, keeping them in his memory (I, 160). They are thus lost to posterity.

It is interesting to note that Proust once wrote of Ruskin that in order to create his work he had sacrificed all his pleasures, all his duties and even his very life.[21] The wording of Proust's statement implies that any real artist must do the very same thing. One would have expected Vinteuil to ignore his daughter's behavior, or to send her away to a school or convent and proceed with his own creative work. But this was not the case; we are told that the composer sacrifices his work, which was his only reason for living, to raise this one daughter after losing his wife (I, 159-160).

The "deciphering" of Vinteuil's papers raises more questions than it answers. The interpreter transforms the unintelligible notations into a musical score because of her familiarity with the composer's work. During her stay in his household she had heard him working out his ideas at the piano and this enables her to reconstruct his compositions. It is then a matter of orchestrating this music, an extraordinary feat for someone who has not "cultivated her musical gift" (I, 147). The deciphered scores, however excellent, are only an approximation of Vinteuil's work. The lady cannot, of course, foresee its development and evolution; she is guided by her idea of his style, fashioning a reproduction, a pastiche of what the composer had played. She reconstructs Vinteuil's work based on his past achievement. The lady is a sorcerer's apprentice who has learned the formulas, transcribing the illegible notations in a style she learned perhaps too well.

The idea that someone can imitate a style so well is disturbing. It implies that unless we have special inside information we cannot tell an original from a copy. It also implies that the imitated artist had a manner rather than a style; style, by definition, is more fluid, changeable, unpredictable, and therefore inimitable. The lady had not only taken the master's daughter but the formula for his work as well. The only thing Proust denies her is a name of her own, perhaps to show that the real credit belongs to Vinteuil, although the transcriber of his notes and of the compositions he had played on the piano certainly accomplished a miracle.

Works of art produced by imitators of a style tend to diminish the importance and the value we attach to originality. The work of Miss Vinteuil's friend is partly original. She may have used some of her own "ideals" or concepts as well as the considerable skills and talent required for orchestration. Because there exists only one piece from the composer's hand, the *Sonata* published during his lifetime, it is difficult for Vinteuil's listeners to separate his achievement from the contribution of his daughter's friend. When he reads Bergotte's books, the narrator asks himself if the differences between works by different artists are due to the efforts or technical skill of the creators rather than to a "radical difference in the essence of personalities" (I, 549). But this question cannot shake his confidence that every original artist shows us a unique world inaccessible by any other means.

In the last few pages of *Remembrance of Things Past*, we are made more strongly aware of the narrator's anguish as he realizes that in his youth, when he was strong, he had neither a subject nor the experience and insight he would acquire during his life. As he nears old age and becomes weak and ill, he feels ever more keenly that his mind is like a mine filled with varied strata of precious materials (III, 1037). His anxiety as to whether he will live long enough to carry out the task of extracting these materials increases when he thinks of the fragility of his health, of the capriciousness of circumstances, and of the inevitability of death. The narrator, in anguish about whether or not he will be able to carry out the work he feels he can now write, states that his strength is no longer equal to the terrible exigencies of his work (III, 1042). He realizes that the work will require continual sacrifices on his part and hopes he will live long enough to make these sacrifices. From the recollections of Proust's friends, it is evident that the narrator's anguish about living long enough to complete his work was exactly the same as that felt by Proust himself. His friend Gauthier-Vignal quotes a letter from the novelist to the painter Jacques-Emile Blanche on the anxiety he suffered.[22]   Like his narrator, he considered himself a sick man, whose strength was declining every day.

He worried that he had begun writing so late that his talent and memory would diminish at the moment he needed them most. For a writer whose goal was to resuscitate the past in its texture and density, the fear of failing memory was a nightmare. Although the imaginary and the imagined play a great role in *Remembrance of Things Past*, biographies of Proust and the recollections of his friends and acquaintances show that his memory of actual, experienced events also had a very large part in his work. His anxieties transformed his life into a race against the clock. One can only hope that the strong disappointment Bergotte feels about his work when he goes to see the Vermeer exhibit was not also experienced by Proust, who attended an exhibit of that painter's work about eighteen months before his death. But a comment he made to his housekeeper when he came home from the exhibit shows that he too felt some of the anguish he attributed to Bergotte. Proust told his housekeeper that his writing didn't have the finish he had seen in Vermeer's paintings.

Like his narrator, Proust believed that originality was the most important element in the work of art. He made this clear in a short article entitled "Sur le monde mystérieux de Gustave Moreau." He remarks that works of art are like "fragmentary glimpses" of their makers' soul, which is like a country unknown to them.[23]   We can only learn anything of this unknown country by understanding the work of art. Unfortunately for its creator, he cannot penetrate at will into the native land of his mind and heart. He is in exile from his own deepest inner self and can never stay in it long enough to explore it a leisure (*CSB*, p. 670).   This simile implies that the artist does not have the power to stay in touch with the essential part of himself. He has no control of it but must take whatever bits and pieces he can snatch, often in a haphazard manner. Like most exiles, he is sad, nostalgic and lonely; he has to adjust to this unhappy situation (*CSB*, p. 672). Proust's comparison also suggests that each artist has his own inner country, totally unlike anyone else's.

In *Contre Sainte-Beuve*, Proust reinforces this idea of the irreducible difference among original artists when he writes that for each one it is always as if he were the first ever to create, as if he were in the same situation as Homer thousands of years ago (*CSB*, 220).   The artist cannot even know what constitutes his originality because he must submit to his subject and attempt to draw nearer to a truth he feels only obscurely (*CSB*, 140-141).   This is why Proust's narrator thinks he has no subject to write about.   Instead of waiting to feel the right one, he tries to arrive at it by means of his intelligence.   But it can be found only by dint of listening to an inner voice or conviction which brings the artist a notion of what he must try to do.

The situation of the artist as Proust described it in "Mélanges," in the article on Moreau and in *Contre Sainte-Beuve*, is the same one his narrator faces.   He too feels threatened with impotence, distraught over what he considers his lack of originality and even of a subject.   It takes the narrator a lifetime to learn what Proust already knew when he was translating Ruskin in 1904, and stated in a note to his translation of *Sesame and Lilies:* "We cannot receive the truth from anybody else, we have to create it ourselves."[24]

The narrator implies that originality is a transitory aspect of a work, at least from the reader's point of view.   A time comes when the narrator admires Bergotte's books much less because they have become too clear.   He has become used to their style, has assimilated their substance, and now must look elsewhere for a different way of seeing.   A page later, he explains that Bergotte having written everything he had it within him to write, is exhausted and leads "a vegetative life" (II, 328).   (The same thing happens to Balzac's artists and thinkers: their work wears them out until finally they are no more than shadows of their former selves).

Pathetic as this passage on Bergotte is, it implies clearly that the artist must give every ounce of vitality to his art, even though it is unlikely to equal what he had hoped to accomplish.   The work of art may also be assimilated and outgrown by its audience.   The only way the work can live is, of course, by attracting new readers.   Bergotte's work dies before he does; he is so spent towards the end that he no longer even reads anything and does not have the energy to envy those who with their new books are eclipsing his own.

To his friend Madame Strauss, Proust wrote that only through original works can we recover the freshness of our impressions and our desire to read (*Corr.* IX, 163).   Only through

writing can the narrator get in touch with himself, with his authentic impressions. Reason made him repress them but
through art he hopes to recreate them and with them his whole
past. The narrator learns through experience that neither love
for, nor suffering caused by, another person can give us the
understanding we gain through art. For this reason he states
that each artist is the citizen of an unknown homeland—his
work (II, 257), and that there are as many different worlds to discover as there are original artists (III, 896).

Proust insisted that the creative self is different from the
everyday self. As the narrator's comments on Vinteuil show,
Proust believed that the artist cannot have any consciousness of
this deeper, more essential, creative self (III, 257). It is unknown
to him, so distant and almost totally inaccessible that it clearly
cannot be the one which functions in everyday life. The narrator knows something Swann could not bring himself to believe.
Vinteuil, the timid, unprepossessing piano teacher of Combray,
is also the composer of the extraordinary, unforgettable music
that Swann, the narrator and the general public admire so un-
reservedly.

For Proust originality meant the ability of certain artists to
transform appearance, to show us another view of the world,
one we would not know if they had not composed, painted or
written. Their power is so great that once we see what they have
seen we are changed. The original artist makes us undergo a
metamorphosis. For this reason the narrator states that Renoir
changed the way people saw the world around them (II, 327).
Elstir's roses are a new variety, unknown before he painted
them; he enriched the rose species (II, 943).

****

A number of artists have destroyed works of their youth.
Among them were the painters Léger, Arp, Nicolas de Staël and
Francis Bacon, the writers Boris Pasternak, Borges, and Max
Frisch and the composers Gustav Mahler and Arnold Schönberg.
Each of these artists believed that in his early works he had not
found his own voice, but was imitating others, or treading a beat-
en path. (This was the explanation given by Arp).[25] Léger stated
that he had destroyed his early work because he felt the coming

to prominence of Cubism and did not want to be associated with a style of painting about to disappear. He later regretted his action.[26] Gauguin wrote to the dealer Ambroise Vollard that of his painting "one hundred do not count because they were immature works."[27]

The case of Martin du Gard is quite typical of a creative individual who destroyed works not representative of his talent. In 1901, at the age of twenty, he wrote his first novel, entitled "La Chrysalide" (The Chrysalis), while a student at the Ecole des Chartes. He abandoned and then destroyed this work because he felt he had undertaken a project too difficult for him. He thought he had not been successful in portraying the heroine as he was not mature or knowledgeable enough to create a woman as a main character. He wrote in August 1901: "Who am I to create a woman?"[28] He noted that he also had difficulties in sorting out personal thoughts, in distinguishing between what he had observed of the world around him and what he owed to his reading. The fear that he could not organize and blend these elements assailed him while he was writing this first novel. He also realized that he should not have transported his two protagonists to a "desert island" away from the pressures of daily life. He was afraid that he had not placed his characters squarely in the mainstream of life.

Claude Sicard in his monumental *Roger Martin du Gard: Les années d'apprentissage littéraire (1881-1910)* notes another factor that gave Martin du Gard considerable difficulty. This was the handling of the religious question: the plot involves a husband's attempt to lead his wife away from the practice of Catholicism. (The theme of the trauma resulting from abandoning religious belief was to recur in much of Martin du Gard's later work). The fledgling novelist found it extremely difficult to deal with this subject. These factors explain his decision to abandon "La Chrysalide."[29]

In early 1903, he began writing a work provisionally entitled "Le Soldat Flers" (The Soldier Flers) based upon an incident he had witnessed while doing his military service. Claude Sicard notes that here too the novelist's literary ambition was greater than his technical skill at the time, and that Martin du Gard's friends discouraged him from writing a novella in dialogue form. This might have been one of the factors leading the novelist to abandon "Jean Flers." Martin du Gard eventually destroyed all the drafts of this work except for two sheets from the original manuscript. In 1903 he wrote another novel, "La Méprise" (The Mistake), which he also destroyed. Sicard, who was able to reconstruct its plot after consulting notes taken by a friend of the novelist's, concluded that there was too great a discrepancy between the young novelist's ambition, ability and personal experience.[30]

Having destroyed his first three manuscripts, Martin du Gard worked on a short novel entitled "Il est d'exquises fleurs" (There are Exquisite Flowers) in 1905. Sicard was able to interview friends of the novelist's who remembered reading the unfinished manuscript of this fourth work. Based on these interviews, he concluded that this short piece showed a great development of the author's sensibility.

Remarks the young novelist made to friends at this time are very revealing. He told Marcel de Coppet that both Benjamin Constant and Eugène Fromentin suffered from being unable to escape from their own personalities.[31] Whether or not Martin du Gard was afraid of suffering the same fate as these predecessors, it is most likely that he thought he had not yet acquired the ability to transport himself into the souls of his characters, who were all too much in his own image. Marcel de Coppet wrote a rather critical letter to his friend upon reading "Il est d'exquises fleurs" and the novelist accepted the criticism well, feeling it was sound. He evidently felt once again that he could not overcome the problems the work presented for he eventually destroyed it too.[32]

In March 1906, at the age of twenty-five, having already undergone a five-year literary apprenticeship with nothing to show for it, Martin du Gard undertook a novel entitled "Une Vie de Saint" (A Saint's Life); he worked on it long and hard for two years before abandoning it, but this time he did not destroy what he had written (the drafts are now in the Bibliothèque Nationale in Paris). He knew from the moment he began the book that the subject—the life story of a small town priest—was too vast. There are sixty characters and the action takes place over a period of sixty years. He wrote a draft of the book, was dissatisfied with it and decided to redo everything (*Corr.* 1, 109). This explanation, in a letter to a close friend, brought a howl of despair from the latter, who pleaded with Martin du Gard not to destroy a work to which he had devoted eight months. The novelist wrote back that he did not have the courage to destroy what he had written, but would instead correct, add to, tighten and strengthen the manuscript (*Corr.* 1, 110).

While he was in the process of doing this, he wrote to Pierre Rain that a battalion of new ideas had come to him and that he faced the problem of integrating them with the already existing manuscript. These revisions caused him a good deal of anxiety as he was not certain that he could carry them out successfully (*Corr.* 1, 111). He complained that the work of a novelist was particularly frustrating because in creative work one could not rely on one's effort or will and there was no known recipe for continuing on the right track (*Corr.* 1, 111-112). He believed that the artist has no means of acting upon himself; two years later he was to write that in art one doesn't know what one is doing, that there is a subconscious force leading the artist on and as a result his work is, on the whole, in conformity with his temperament (*Corr.* 1, 130). Martin du Gard finally decided to redo the prologue of "Une Vie de Saint" and resolved to rewrite the entire childhood and adolescence of his protagonist to show everyday life in the provinces as experienced by the characters who surround the hero (*Corr.* 1, 112-113). But two weeks later he wrote to a friend that the entire section dealing with life in the provinces needed to be redone completely. He thought it would be much better if he did not look at the existing drafts at all, and decided to start again from scratch. He thought it would be better to "reincarnate" the character of the town doctor, to put various characters in the forefront together with his hero so that the depiction of life in the provincial town would become more vivid. But at the end of 1907, he began to question his work seriously and realized that he could not hope to accomplish what he had been so sure of doing only a month earlier (*Corr.* 1, 116-117). He decided accordingly to abandon "Une Vie de Saint" altogether, feeling he had not wasted his time completely as he had learned a great deal from his labors. He made further desperate attempts to continue reworking it, but, not accomplishing anything worthwhile, he finally abandoned it for good in the Spring of 1908.

He had published nothing as yet and had destroyed almost everything he had done up to this point. He felt that he needed to write and publish a work very quickly in order to prove to himself that he was indeed a writer. In the Spring of 1908 he began to work on a novel entitled *Devenir* (Becoming) which was published in June 1909, with the author paying for its publication. The young novelist exorcised his previous failures in writing this book, whose subject was the life of a young but failed novelist. The book received some very good reviews and Martin du Gard was launched on his career.

In July 1909 he began working on a novel later to be entitled "Marise." Its subject would be a major crisis in the life of a woman, an event causing a psychological upheaval in the heroine's principles, education and beliefs. A few weeks later, on September 10, 1909, he wrote to a friend that he had thrown out two hundred fifty pages of outlines and drafts for this novel and had finally written a new outline with which he was satisfied (*Corr.* 1, 139). Three weeks later, on October first 1909, he wrote to another friend that his project was giving him much trouble. Although the subject was splendid and very human, there was a terrible gap between it and the actual writing he was doing, which he called "navrant" (calamitous) (*Corr.* 1, 140). On December 2, 1909, he wrote to a third friend that he had already written five times the number of pages that his work would have in the end, but complained that all the preparatory work consisting of outlines, drafts, notes was worthless and would have to be burned. It is not clear from the correspondence whether Martin du Gard was referring to the first two hundred fifty pages he had thrown out in September 1909 or whether he was throwing out the outline and notes redone after he discarded the first two hundred and fifty pages of preparatory work. In April 1910, he decided to abandon this novel; he kept only one hundred pages, which he published as a novella under the title *L'Une de nous* (One of us). In the *Correspondance 1*, he states that *L'Une de nous* was a fragment of a novel he had almost entirely completed. In "Souvenirs autobiographiques et littéraires" he states that he had only written two hundred fifty pages of preliminary notes and drafts which were useless and had to be destroyed but that he had not started writing the novel itself.[33] It is rather hard to believe that he could have forgotten that he had almost finished a novel and destroyed all but one hundred pages of it. It may be that in "Souvenirs auto-biographiques et littéraires" he did not want to present all the details of his earlier failure.

In November 1913, at 32, Martin du Gard published his first major work, *Jean Barois*. His lack of self-confidence continued, however. He felt a hesitancy about the direction he should take. Letters written in 1918 show that he was pulled in different directions by his instincts on the one hand and by his intellect and training in scientific documentation on the other.

He could not trust his instincts since he felt, as many artists have, that such trust leads to the easy way and then causes one to become imprisoned within one's subjectivity. Very early in his career, he had quoted a statement by the essayist Alain: "The first law is to doubt what one likes."[34] The same idea also occurred to Marcel Duchamp and led him to say: "I forced myself to contradict myself in order to avoid conforming to my own taste."[35] He repeated this later in an interview.[36]

The painter Robert Rauschenberg destroyed one hundred fifty silk screen paintings as "a form of insurance against the pressure to repeat himself."[37]   The danger of becoming a prisoner of one's taste and technical skill is one that many artists are acutely aware of, but not all have had the courage to stop themselves from falling into this trap.   It is precisely for this courage and this sense of integrity that a perceptive critic praised Jacques Rivière when he wrote, in 1925, that this novelist and critic knew how to think against himself.[38]

In addition to fear of his own subjectivity, and of what brought him "joy through effort," Martin du Gard felt that his intellectual bent was making him swerve from the spontaneous individuality that was his real element.[39]   He was intensely "preoccupied" by the moral, economic and social issues of his time; the novel of ideas interested him very greatly as did the interaction of contemporary problems, ideas and emotions in the lives of his characters.   He was most uneasy about the compromise that had to be made in weaving these strands into the fabric of the novels.   This was because the personal, original element seemed to him to be drowning under the weight of those sociological and ideological problems facing his characters. His work therefore appeared to him dry, artificial, lifeless.   By compromising and trying to interweave both the personal and historical elements, he thought he was making a mistake which would diminish the value of his work.   Yet he could not definitely opt for either tendency.[40]   As he worked, he instinctively felt that he was committing a great blunder.   The feeling of being pulled in different directions was to continue throughout his career, together with misgivings about his attempts to compromise and to steer a middle course.

In a letter of March 12, 1918, he noted how difficult it was to know oneself, and this difficulty increased his fear of being mistaken in choosing the right course.   If one cannot ever know oneself, then how can one be certain of having chosen the right course to follow? (*Corr.* 11, 228).   It is ironic of course, that Martin du Gard, so highly praised for his acccurate depiction of French society between the two World Wars, should have felt that this very aspect of his work might prevent him from becoming the kind of novelist he wanted to be.

It is also apparent from his letter of March 12, 1918 that one of his problems was a fear that, like Constant, Flaubert and Fromentin, he would not know how to go outside of himself and put himself into the soul of another being. Yet he was also convinced that, to be an artist, one must fully develop in oneself what is unique (*Corr.* 11, 228). This fear of not being able to feel what another human being feels was heightened by another —that he did not have the imagination needed to help him across the divide between himself and others. Letting his imagination roam was impossibly difficult for him: he needed the support of situations he had experienced, places where he had lived and people he had known well.[41]

The first-hand experience of having written and destroyed six novels did not mean that Martin du Gard had learned to solve the problems he would face in the future.   But the apprenticeship of ten years of working and thinking did teach him a great deal; this is clear from the fact that he was able to write *Jean Barois* in just under three years. This novel, published in November 1913, the same month as the first two volumes of Proust's novel, was not a great success at the time. But its author gained self-confidence due to congratulatory letters sent by half a dozen very famous writers whose approval would have made any novelist quite proud.

In the Spring of 1920, barely recovered from the emotional experiences he had undergone at the front, Martin du Gard began to work on *Les Thibault,* a novel dealing with the life of two brothers. After finishing the first volume he showed it to a very close friend, Marcel de Coppet, who criticized the work for lacking the "spark" of originality, the individuality or the "natural spontaneity" its author showed in his letters and conversations.   This must have been demoralizing for the author of *Les Thibault,* who was constantly reproaching himself for the very same reasons. His publisher, Gaston Gallimard, complained of his too obvious attempts at trying to be a *styliste,* which resulted only in artificiality.   (Martin du Gard's friend André Gide made the same criticism). Gallimard also objected to the overly long descriptions, which, he felt, interrupted the flow of the narrative, a judgment also expressed by another friend, the novelist Georges Duhamel.[42]   Martin du Gard revised the first two volumes of *Les Thibault* in the light of these criticisms but luckily did not destroy these volumes.   As of the time he began writing this novel, he had not yet overcome the sense of hesitancy which had previously prevented him from letting himself go and from trusting his imagination and "natural spontaneity," to use de Coppet's phrase.

He continued to work on his novel.   He was often discouraged and had doubts about its worth.   He had a particularly difficult time with the volume entitled "L'Appareillage" (Setting Sail) on which he worked in 1929-1930.   On January 1, 1931, he and his wife were both severely injured in a car accident and hospitalized.   While immobilized in the hospital, he began to have very grave doubts about the seventh volume of his novel, "L'Appareillage," of which the first half was ready to go to press.   He feared that by hewing to the plan settled on back in 1920, he was seriously jeopardizing the "unity and equilibrium of the whole work."[43]   He attempted to change his outline, to cut it, and to rework it, but after long hesitations decided he would have to abandon the 1920 plan and replace it with another.   He concluded that the seventh volume, on which he had spent nearly two years, would slow the plot too much and would be better omitted.   He burned "L'Appareillage" in 1931 so that he would not be tempted to go back on his decision.[44]

After this incident, it took Martin du Gard four years to get back to the point where he could feel confident of integrating the first six volumes with those he was then working on.   The anxiety that the second part of the novel caused its author can be seen in the letters he wrote to Gide between August 1933 and September 1935.   The worst problem facing him was what he called his total "désaffection" toward the book, a feeling of more than indifference, so that he had to fight with himself to sit down and continue writing.   He felt that his characters were dead, and that he had to resuscitate them.   After changing his plan and setting aside the manuscript for three years, he found it almost impossible to plunge back into the life of the characters. He was so discouraged that he considered abandoning the novel completely and wondered if this would be worse than continuing a book for which he had lost all feeling.   It had become a *pensum* or unpleasant obligation.[45]

He again stated that his problems were caused in large

part by his inability to rely solely on his inner self and on his feelings for the subject; he had to feel objectively, as if detached from himself.   The characters whose life he had to create appeared to him to be "ghosts" of those in the previous volumes.[46] The interweaving of the life of his characters with the historical reality of 1914 also overwhelmed him, and he was not sure he could even make the effort to compose the grid that underpinned the narrative.[47]   In June 1934, he complained to Gide that he no longer had enough "breadth, . . . flexibility, . . . perspective" and that moreover he had neither the memory nor the ability required to form an overview of the book.   He described himself as a miniaturist who, with his tiny brush, had undertaken to paint a fresco.[48]

All this self-doubt and anguish was caused by exhaustion. When he recovered from the injuries sustained in the 1931 accident, he not only began thinking about a total revision of the plan of *Les Thibault*, but also worked on a play and a short novel.   His play, *Un Taciturne*, appeared in 1932 and the novella was published in 1933 under the title *Vieille France* (Old France). The three volumes of *L'Eté 1914* (The Summer of 1914) were published in November 1936 followed in 1940 by the final volume of *Les Thibault*, entitled *Epilogue*.   Clearly Martin du Gard was not wasting time or suffering from writer's block.   He sounded pessimistic in his letters to Gide no doubt because other problems, mainly monetary ones, were causing him a great deal of worry.   But there is no question about his excessive severity toward himself and his work. He was a very stern taskmaster.

The problem Martin du Gard faced beginning in 1931 following completion of the first six volumes of *Les Thibault* is one familiar to artists who work on one project for a long time—lagging interest. It is understandably quite difficult to fix upon a plan and work according to it for eighteen years, as Martin du Gard attempted to do.   It was inevitable that he himself and his attitude would change during the years he spent on the novel. Such changes were bound to modify his view of the work and of the direction he had established for himself in 1920. He wrote to Gide on December 2, 1930, that the story he had invented had little by little lost its fictive character. The plot had become so certain that it could no more be modified than a historical event can be modified in retrospect. He felt that his work was practically that of a historian, rather than of a writer. The plan drawn up in 1920 irritated him because of its increasing rigidity.

Not until the aftermath of the 1931 car accident did he ever consider departing from this plan.   To do so would undoubtedly have caused gaps and possibly confusion in the narrative, and would have been detrimental to the unity and verisimilitude of the novel (elements of the utmost importance to him). He concluded his letter to Gide by noting that he was condemned to tell what had happened to his characters even if that ceased to interest him. He felt that he had no choice if he did not want to give up *Les Thibault* altogether.   He was too deeply involved with the work to set it aside, and it represented a great investment of emotional and intellectual energy. Luckily he found the determination to finish the work and was rewarded for his labors with the Nobel Prize for literature in November 1937.

In 1940, Martin du Gard began work on what would be his last novel, left unfinished, "Le Journal du Colonel de Maumort." He had considerable difficulty in reconstituting the historical background of the year 1940 when his hero, a retired military officer, began his diary and reflected on the events around him. The novelist started this work with overwhelming enthusiasm and wrote to Gide that he found the days too short. He said he wished he could shut himself in a Benedictine abbey to work with all his might until his last days on earth. He found his work more satisfying because he was in that blessed planning stage prior to the actual writing.[49]

After two years of preparatory work, he began to have doubts as to whether he had made the right choice in using the memoir form in a first person narrative. He thought that it prevented him from showing characters in action and from using what he called his most natural gifts. He then envisaged the possiblity of presenting Maumort's life in a series of novellas. They would take their unity from the fact that Colonel Maumort was to be the hero of all of them, and the same characters would reappear.   But Martin du Gard was also conscious that this genre required sacrifices he was not sure he wanted to make. Beginning in October 1943 his attention to his work began to wane, and he concentrated instead on the real-life drama of the war; he ended up by not believing in his own novel any more.[50]

Martin du Gard was now an old man who, in his own view, had undertaken a work too ambitious for him.   His vitality was declining and he thought it foolish to try to write a work he wouldn't have been able to manage at the height of his powers; he noted that within him a spring had snapped. He was grateful that he still had the lucidity to see things as they were. Yet he did not give up hope that with a certain amount of rewriting Le Journal du Colonel de Maumort might be salvageable. He also attempted in 1946, to write a play about the youth of the time but abandoned this project, deciding that he was too old for such a subject.[51]

When the war ended, Martin du Gard went back to his novel. He realized that the perspective in which he had written had been influenced far too much by the war years. To change the perspective, he decided that his hero's diary should begin in 1945 instead of around 1941 or 1942, but this would entail recasting the whole plot.[52] From 1947 to 1952, he continued to work on the novel. At times he was disappointed, but with Gide's continued encouragement, he found the impetus to continue it. Failing memory and strength finally compelled him to abandon the novel. It was published posthumously in 1983 under the title Le Lieutenant-Colonel de Maumort.

The letters he wrote in 1917 and 1918 to his friend Jacques Rivière, the editor of the Nouvelle Revue Française, show that Martin du Gard was torn by fears and indecision. He wanted above all to be original, to contribute what he felt to be uniquely his own. His most personal gift was for the creation of believable characters having the full vigor and variety of life. But he found that whenever he sat down to write a novel, he overloaded it with political, sociological and historical considerations. The characters he created were thereby eclipsed. It was as if the setting became more important than the portrait. He was also afraid that he didn't have the breadth and depth of experience or the understanding to create an authentic world of his own. Unfortunately for his ego, he kept thinking of Tolstoy's example, and this naturally discouraged him as he knew he was not a writer of that class. His letters to Rivière also show that Martin du Gard felt he had arrived at a crossroads and needed to make a decision as to which of the aspects of the novel he would henceforth concentrate on. He seemed to be on the verge of choosing the "oeuvre de sensibilité," which he judged to be his forte. He thought of giving up the "oeuvre d'idées" because other writers could, after all, handle ideas as well as he. He knew that either of these choices would change his life as each demanded a different way of working, another approach, style and frame of mind. But a choice would also mean closing off the other alternative for good.

His letters to Rivière are moving testimony of the novelist's need to confide in a sympathetic listener; they remind us of the letters in which Flaubert unburdened himself to Louis Bouilhet and others. Martin du Gard knew that he would have to make the choice alone, and his letters to his friend were an attempt to find the strength to finally make the decision. His case only points up the fact that no artist knows where his originality really lies, and goes through enormous torment until he finds his own way. Many destroy their work because they have not found their real direction, or what is worse, mistakenly believe they have not found it or remain unhappy with it because they had dreamed of something else.

Proust believed so strongly in originality that he felt the modern writer was in the same situation as Homer centuries ago. He thought that a writer can learn little from others, and must rely largely on a meditation on his own experience, on what he has felt. Flaubert spoke for all three when he noted that for every new work a new poetics is necessary; skill gained from working on a previous book is useless as each new piece is an entirely new challenge.

It is quite likely that Flaubert wanted to become "the other," as that was one of the few ways to forget one's own personality. This forgetting was as essential to him as it was to Proust and Proust's narrator and to Roger Martin du Gard. The latter feared that he might never escape the prison of his personality or become another being through the creation of believable characters. He too was sure that only by getting into another's skin could he hope to understand a world different from his own.

At the end of *Remembrance of Things Past* the narrator seems less fearful than either Flaubert or Martin du Gard of not knowing how to create fully-rounded characters. He was more concerned with the possibility that he might not know how to make his readers feel that his story was also theirs, "that the passions of one are the passions of all" (III, 907). He was apprehensive that readers might not be able to generalize from the experience of one or several characters to extract truths which he considered widely applicable. If readers do not derive greater insight and self-understanding when they read his work, then the novelist, of course, has failed in his endeavor. He must not only move others but bring them perceptions and insights they could not attain in any other way. In spite of all his self-doubts, an artist still needs to feel that in some way he has made a difference. He often thinks that if he does not fashion a work which only he can produce, some aspect of human experience would not be brought to light. This is why Wordsworth stated that it would be a shame for him to waste his talent. He had to share it with others because he was a witness to a reality important to them.

Notes

1 Gustave Flaubert, *Correspondance*, 13 vols. (Paris: Conard-Lambert, 1926-1954), II, 345. All references to the *Correspondance* are to this edition.

2 Maurice Bardèche, *L'Oeuvre de Flaubert* (Paris: Les Sept Couleurs, 1974), p. 179.

3 *Writers at Work*, second series (New York: Viking Press, 1973), p. 126.

4 Quoted by Ian Dunlop, *The Shock of the New* (New York: American Heritage Press, 1971), p. 82.

5 Quoted by Jean Paulhan, *Oeuvres complètes*, 5 vols. (Paris: Cercle du livre précieux, 1970), V, 244-245.

6 Joachim Gasquet, *Cézanne* (Paris: 1921), p. 94.

7 Gasquet, p. 90.

8 Quoted in *Le Monde*, June 7, 1981, p. 11.

9 *Writers at Work*, second series (New York: Viking Press, 1963), p. 272.

10 *The Collected Letters of Joseph Conrad*, ed. F. R. Karl and L. Davis, (New York: Cambridge University Press, 1983), vol. I (1861-1897), p. 171. This remark was made in a letter dated August 1894.

11 André Breton, *Le Point du jour* (Paris: Gallimard, 1970), p. 9.

12 *Mémoires d'un fou*, *Oeuvres de Gustave Flaubert*, 2 vols. (Paris: Gallimard-Pléiade, 1951-1952), II, 468.

13 Werner Hoffman, "Marcel Duchamp and Emblematic Realism," in *Marcel Duchamp: Perspectives*, ed. Joseph Masheck (Englewood Cliffs, N.J., Prentice-Hall, Inc., 1975), p. 59.

14 Quoted by Jérôme Garcin, "Romain Gary," *1981 Universalia* (Paris: Encyclopaedia Universalis, 1982), pp. 551-552.

15 Bernard Pingaud, "Omega," *Nouvelle Revue de Psychologie*, no. 14 (1976), p. 257.

16 Gérard Genette, *Figures I* (Paris: Editions du Seuil, 1966), 235.

17 *Carnet 1908*, ed. Philip Kolb (Paris: Gallimard, 1976), p. 61. This book will hereafter be referred to as *C 1908*.

18 Quoted in Maurice Bardèche, *Marcel Proust romancier*, 2 vols. (Paris: Les Sept Couleurs, 1971), II, 410.

19 Quoted in Bardèche, II, 406.

20 Quoted in Bardèche, II, 407.

21 "Mélanges," *Contre Sainte-Beuve* (Paris: Gallimard-Pléiade, 1971), p. 76.

22 Gauthier-Vignal, *Proust connu et inconnu* (Paris: Editions Robert Laffont, 1976), pp. 69, 132.

23 *Contre Sainte-Beuve*, p. 670.

24 "Journées de lecture," *Contre Sainte-Beuve*, pp. 792-793.

25 Jean Clay, *Visages de l'art moderne* (Lausanne: Editions Rencontre, 1969), p. 20.

26 André Verdet, *Entretiens, notes et écrits sur la peinture* (Paris: Galilee, 1978), p. 59.

27 *Letters to Ambroise Vollard and André Fontainas*, p. 35.

28 Roger Martin du Gard, *Correspondance Générale*, ed. Maurice Rieuneau, (Paris: Gallimard, 1980), I (1896-1913), 61.

29 Claude Sicard, *Roger Martin du Gard: Les années d'apprentissage littéraire - 1881-1910* (Lille: Université de Lille III, H. Champion, 1976), pp. 117-118.

30 Sicard, pp. 131, 133, 151, 155.

31 Sicard, p. 160.

32 Sicard, p. 157-158.

33 Roger Martin du Gard, *Correspondance Générale*, I, p. 182. "Souvenirs autobiographiques et littéraires" a short autobiography by Martin du Gard appears as an introduction to the Pléiade edition of his work.

34 André Gide, Roger Martin du Gard, *Correspondance*, 2 vols. (Paris: Gallimard, 1968), I (1913-1934), 637.

35 Quoted in Calvin Tomkins, *Off the Wall* (New York: Doubleday & Co., Inc., 1980), p. 275.

36 Pierre Cabanne, *Conversations with Marcel Duchamp* (New York: Viking Press, 1971), pp. 48, 94.

37 Calvin Tomkins, p. 235.

38 Charles Du Bos, *Approximations* (Paris: Fayard, 1965), p. 477.

39 Roger Martin du Gard, "Lettres à Jacques Rivière," *Nouvelle Revue Française*, décembre 1958, p. 1122.

40 "Lettres à Jacques Rivière," p. 1118-1122.

41 Lettres à Jacques Rivière," p. 1123-1127.

42 Roger Martin du Gard, "Souvenirs autobiographiques et littéraires," I, pp. lxxxii-lxxxiv.

43 "Souvenirs," p. xcvi.

44 "Souvenirs," p. xcviii.

45 *Correspondance Gide-Martin du Gard*, I, 571-572.

46 *Correspondance Gide-Martin du Gard*, I, 571-573.

47 *Correspondance Gide-Martin du Gard*, I, 580.

48 Ibid., p. 622.

49 "Souvenirs autobiographiques et littéraires," p. cxii-cxiv.

50 "Souvenirs," p. cxxi.

51 "Souvenirs," p. cxxix.

52 "Souvenirs," p. cxxx.

Unfinished Near-Masterpieces:

The Prelude, like *Remembrance of Things Past* is the story of the formation and development of an artist and also describes the stages he undergoes in the creation of his work. While Proust compares his novel to a cathedral, Wordsworth compares *The Prelude* to the "portico," then to the "ante-chapel," of a gothic church; the unfinished poem *The Recluse* was to be its nave. Both writers created their work through a process of innumerable rewritings, revisions, additions and corrections, over a period of fifty years in Wordsworth's case and about twenty-six years in Proust's. They often felt a lack of confidence, a sense of frustration sometimes combined with a feeling of despair at not being able to accomplish what they dreamed of. Robert Musil and Arrigo Boito also experienced these emotions in their unsuccessful efforts to finish their major works.

Like Proust, Wordsworth and Musil believed that art was not an activity to be engaged in solely to fulfill the artist's needs, or for his own pleasure, but that it must have a purpose or principle transcending the life of the individual artist and any of his works. A great deal of soul-searching ensued for all three; defining this transcendent purpose was not an easy task and probably caused interruptions in their work as well as a drawn-out search for an intellectually satisfying foundation on which to base it. When an artist cannot find such a principle for his work he may spend much time and energy trying to create one for himself, or he may abandon the work. Proust and Wordsworth both did this, although Proust abandoned his novel *Jean Santeuil* (published posthumously in 1952) only to take up most of its themes in *Remembrance of Things Past*.

If the artist doubts that he has a governing principle or a foundation for his work, he may spend considerable time wondering if he will ever write anything and whether he is an artist at all. Like the narrator of his novel, Proust spent years searching for some certainty or directing principle and according to some critics may not have found a very solid one. Maurice

Blanchot, among others, has wondered if the importance Proust attached to privileged moments, or "spots of time" (to use Wordsworth's phrase) was sufficient to support the weight placed on them.[1] It is not clear whether either Proust or Wordsworth ever concluded that there is no transcendent intellectual or philosophical principle or value a writer can rely on. Proust believed that each artist creates his own value which constitutes a base to support the weight of his work (III, 895). Wordsworth held a similar belief; he felt a sense of possessing unique individual "knowledge" which he thought it his duty to "impart" so it would not be lost or wasted.[2]

But he had great difficulty in reconciling his thoughts on the personal nature of art with his equally strong convictions that the artist's task or mission is to teach the reader "to see, to think and feel" and to become a better person.[3] He repeated these thoughts in the "Essay Supplementary to the Preface of 1815." He believed that the personal, original element must be subordinated to the artist's role as creator of a work valuable to society. He refused to publish any part of *The Prelude* during his lifetime, because:

> . . . it seems a frightful deal to say about one's self, and of course, will never be published (during my lifetime I mean), till another work has been written and published, of sufficient importance to justify me in giving my own history to the world.[4]

The reason Wordsworth had undertaken *The Prelude* in the first place was that he felt unsure of himself; he was not ready to embark upon a vast poem like *The Recluse* precisely because the intellectual and philosophical basis for this work appeared to him to be too weak. He thought that if he began with a poem describing his own feelings he would be explaining the development and maturation of his own mind and creativity—a subject he believed he knew well. This effort would prepare him to write his philosophical work.[5]

He soon realized that writing a long autobiographical poem was an enterprise fraught with innumerable, unforeseen difficulties. It became apparent to him that he would always have doubts as to the meaning and rationale of what he was doing.[6] This questioning of his purpose and his self-consciousness about his ideas would not let him work without constant self-doubt. For Keats, in contrast to Wordsworth, poetry would need no justification beyond itself, as he believed that: ". . . probably every mental pursuit takes its reality and worth from the ardour of the pursuer—being in itself a nothing—ethereal thing . . ." (Letter of 13 March 1818). But Wordsworth felt obliged to understand and justify the creative process; his self-consciousness led him to wonder about the phenomenon of imagination and how it reacts to stimulation provided by exterior objects.[7]

There is a great deal of similarity between the ideas of Wordsworth and Proust on the role played by exterior objects in creativity as well as on the role of imagination, the importance of art and the very processes of creation. Both believed that some instinct in the writer's personality seizes upon certain objects and invests them with special importance. As a result, the object becomes the reflector of a hidden meaning which it radiates back to the artist, who attempts to elucidate the secret of this meaning (II, 237-270). It soon became clear to Wordsworth that even if there was an emotional link between the poet and the object he was drawn to, this attraction was not enough to sustain artistic creation. In Book III of *The Prelude* he states that the meaning he sought did not lie in an exterior object, no matter how beautiful it was, but in the significance he gave it because it had stirred an emotion in him (III, 130-133).

On January 4, 1810, in a letter published in the review *The Friend*, Wordsworth wrote that the poet's mind, ". . . infusing by meditation into the object with which it converses an intellectual life . . ." creates meaning and a value which lies not in the objects but in the meaning given by the poet.[8] The famous "spots of time" passage implies that the sense of harmony created or found in moments of exaltation has a meaning transcending them (*The Prelude* 1799, 288-294). It must be deciphered or created by the poet as it accounts for the "fructifying virtue" of these moments. The resemblance of Proust's privileged moments to Wordsworth's "spots of time" is quite striking: for both writers the full meaning of such moments can only be made clear by an effort of the mind which acts "by infusing into the objects with which it converses an intellectual life."[9]

For both writers, objects have great importance to the mind because they intimate another, deeper reality behind them. This reality stimulates meditation which later has little need of objects, once it is fully developed and thought and imagination have taken over. As Gilles Deleuze points out in *Proust and Signs*, objects like the hawthorns, the three trees near Hudimesnil, the church spires of Martinville, the tea and the madeleine, are signs pointing to a reality beyond them: only the pursuit of this reality beyond the sign can help the narrator to understand what he had glimpsed fleetingly. The artist alone can create this reality, for it is not in the objects themselves. Wordsworth believed this as well, as the lines of verse in which he speaks of giving "a moral life to every natural form" attest (III, 130-133). He wanted this "moral life" to have a value transcending the work of art.

The tension to be maintained between the individual or personal character of the work and its intellectual value proved to be a major problem for the poet and he could not resolve it to his satisfaction. Perhaps he was made "diffident" by a comparison between his work and a too exalted or awe-inspiring conception of the poetry of his predecessors. Wordsworth denied this possibility in *The Prelude* (VI, 55-62). Other factors are more important in explaining his difficulties. He speaks of his "aspiration toward some philosophic song of Truth" (I, 228-229) and adds that initially he found the burden of this aspiration so heavy that he put off work on the poem with the hope that when he was more mature he would have greater understanding and clearer insight (I, 236-237). In addition to his belief that he lacked the maturity or wisdom needed to undertake a philosophical poem, Wordsworth was also troubled by the realization that his creative impulse was checked by "vague longing, haply bred by want of power" (I, 239). He goes on to accuse himself of not being able to distinguish fear of failure from prudence, and "circumspection" from the constant delays his fear of powerlessness causes him (I, 228-255). In this same passage he adds that he always sees either some "imperfection" in the subject he has chosen, or his own deficiency, and this causes him sadness and depression (I, 255-268).

Wordsworth soon came to the realization that the artist's feelings of inadequacy are inevitable. He, the artist, invariably reaches a stage from which, no matter how his powers and faculties have grown, he can always go far beyond the point he has reached (II, 315-322). Even when the poet was conscious of having the power to work toward the fulfillment of his aspirations, he found much to his chagrin, that it would not always obey him and could not be tamed and controlled (II, 362-368). Often he underwent a torment well known to most artists, because he realized, after rereading something he had judged to be good, that it was very disappointing. He was then unhappy with his work and had to admit that his judgment had been faulty. In a letter dated June 3, 1805, he speaks precisely of the disappointment he experienced on rereading *The Prelude*, the first long work he had completed. He judges it to be "so far below what I seem'd capable of executing" that it "depressed" him. He had numerous experiences of powerlessness during the writing of this poem and one such incident caused an interruption of some years in its composition. Book VII begins by noting that six years have elapsed since the composition of the first half (VII, 4-12). At times he admits that he is not in control of the work (VII, 5-8).

In a letter of March 27, 1821, Dorothy Wordsworth states that her brother believed "unfinished works should not, if it be possible, be left behind."[10] Obviously, the poet wished to complete *The Recluse* but the obstacles that prevented him from doing so were beyond his will to overcome. He writes in *The Prelude* that "hiding places of my power/Seem open, I approach and then they close" (XI, 336-338). These lines show that the approach cannot be voluntary on the poet's part. His writing must not result from any forced or deliberate effort.

The poet also realized that his powers would diminish with age, and that while he was still able to do so, he must restore "the spirit of the Past" (XII, 280-285). His earlier knowledge or intuitions had dimmed and as he tried to recapture his experience he could not do so. Proust's narrator was to have the same feeling when he could not recapture the full meaning and the texture of the past at will either. In Wordsworth's case, aging had an adverse influence on his ability to reach the source of his powers as an artist. In Book XII, he asks to be forgiven for having thought he could join the company of great poets who have a gift for creating enduring works "like one of Nature's" (XII, 1805, 312). Yet *The Prelude* concludes with the poet's ascent of Mount Snowdon, where his doubts about his creative powers disappear and the scene he witnesses on the mountain renews his faith in himself and his ambition to write the poem he envisions (*The Recluse*). Wordsworth had begun work on this poem in 1797-1798. He composed most of the first part, *Home at Grasmere*, in 1800, and another part entitled *The Prospectus* in 1800-1801. He returned to the part entitled *Home at Grasmere* in 1806. Between 1806 and 1814 he worked on a part of the poem entitled *The Excursion* which in 1814, he decided to publish separately: completion of the entire poem seemed very distant.

Between 1814 and the mid 1830's Wordsworth worked very little on *The Recluse*. He gave two reasons for his inability to finish it. He feared he could not do justice to the subject, and with advancing age he was "under a pressure of apprehension" he could not rid himself of.[11] But in fact his problems with *The Recluse* had begun well before he felt too old to resolve them. They dogged him even when he was still young enough to be free of "the pressure of apprehension" attributed to advancing age.

This "pressure of apprehension" was caused by contradictions which Wordsworth labored under and which finally got the better of him. He did not want to publish *The Prelude* because of the "personal nature" of the work. This indicates that *The Recluse* would not be as personal in character as the earlier poem. But in a description of *The Recluse*, he had stated that its subject would be " . . . whatever I find most interesting in Nature, Man, Society, most adapted to Poetic illustration."[12] This sentence shows that the subject of the poem would again be highly personal. He hoped to combine this personal approach with his no less firmly held belief that the poet's task is to teach the reader "to see, to think and feel" so as to become a better person. He added: "There is scarcely one of my Poems which does not aim to direct the attention to some moral sentiment, or to some general principle or law of thought, of our intellectual constitution" (Letter of May 21, 1807, p. 148). In the "Essay Supplementary to the Preface (1815)" he specifically added that a poet, through his work, must make a contribution for "the benefit of human nature."

Wordsworth was either unwilling or unable to admit to himself that his personal, individual reactions and emotions were valuable and had an importance far beyond their seeming subjectivity. He believed that *The Prelude* should be locked away in a drawer as if it were a second-rate work. He was determined that it not be published until he had either died or succeeded in writing a more important long poem, one of a moral or philosophical nature. The irony is that in his time—the heyday of "Romantic" poetry—one would have expected Wordsworth to believe in his own individuality and originality as sources and subjects of his work. Certainly his friend Coleridge believed this: he wrote of Milton, " . . . the sublimest parts of *Paradise Lost* are the revelations of Milton's own mind, producing itself and evolving its own greatness."[13]

As Wordsworth was hesitant to use his own personal experience and instead sought some external truth with a valid intellectual worth of its own, he was caught in a dilemma leading to the suppression of the personal, introspective element. His reluctance to rely on his originality increased "the pressure of apprehension" he felt and led him to abandon *The Recluse*. It is true, of course, that he used his own experience in writing *The Excursion*. Many critics have pointed out that the Pedlar, the Solitary and the Wanderer are aspects of their creator.[14]   The need he felt to subordinate his individuality by presenting recognizable types of people and their problems, led to a work in which the stated goal to present his own views on Man, Nature and Society stood in conflict with his desire to write a philosophical poem with a scope transcending the personal element.

The pressure of writing a philosophical poem like *The Recluse*, which he termed "a more important work" than *The Prelude* of 1805 (Letter of March 5, 1804) is one of the factors which made it impossible for Wordsworth to finish it. Either he could not find a transcendent value for this poem, or he felt that it was beyond his powers to create one, or he was afraid he might relapse into the autobiographical mode of his first long poem. He probably feared that by pursuing too personal a vein he would shut himself into his own subjectivity rather than reach out beyond it.   He was under pressure from himself to write a deeper, wider ranging, and less personal work than *The Prelude*. He had set himself too difficult a task, as he himself admitted in 1838.

Wordsworth also claimed that his past experience, especially the writing of *The Prelude*, had brought him to a point where he believed he was mature enough to undertake a major philosophical poem. If so, the first poem was not as "tributary" or as "subsidiary" as he had stated it to be in the "Preface to the Edition of 1814" and in a letter of March 6, 1804. Knowledge of his past would then be essential to the reader for a better understanding of the history of the author's mind and of the poem written when he had finally found his own voice. He considered his autobiographical poem to be an apprenticeship but did not provide a very clear idea of how writing the first poem gave him the maturity to compose the second. It is not clear whether he meant that maturity had come with the knowledge acquired through experience of life and growing older, or rather through some specific changes brought about within him by the work and reflection that accompanied the writing of *The Prelude*. His comparison of *The Prelude* to a "portico" and then to the "antechapel" of a church is contradictory and raises more questions than it answers; the portico and antechapel are not dispensable parts of a church. It is difficult, if not impossible, to decide from Wordsworth's comments whether he considered *The Prelude* "tributary" (or "subsidiary") to *The Recluse* because it was highly personal, or because it had a less important function.

There is also the problem raised by the fact that posterity has judged *The Prelude* superior to *The Excursion*. It is unclear whether Wordsworth himself felt that his first long poem was better than the second, unfinished one. If so, this may be the reason why he would not allow it to be published after he abandoned *The Recluse*. That would be an admission that the first poem had brought him to a point where he felt sure of his ability to compose his major philosophical work—only to bear the frustration of having to abandon it.

Flaubert's belief in the need for impersonal truth resembles Wordsworth's conviction that the artist's task is to create a "philosophic song of Truth." But both felt that the expression of personal feeling was the necessary first step towards the creation of "philosophical" literature, which they held to be the only worthwhile kind. They feared that the artist's feelings are too restricted, narrow, and changeable, locked into a small world beyond which it is difficult to go. Both thought that the public sought something objectively valuable from art.

The ambivalence felt by both Wordsworth and Flaubert was due to a contradiction. They both sought to create works which could be objectively assessed. Yet their intuition was that perhaps the artist does not in fact produce anything of objective value or meaning. They feared that what the artist produces draws its worth from the sincerity of what he expresses and the intensity with which he conveys his personal emotion. They found it difficult to reconcile their views of what the work of art ought to be with their intuition of what it was for them—an expression of the feelings of a single, inevitably isolated consciousness.

Wordsworth's refusal to publish a highly personal work during his lifetime indicates that for him a personal work could not be "philosophical" and was for that reason of secondary rank. There was obviously a hierarchy of subjects for him; he felt that some were more noble than others and that personal

poems were less important than those with lofty moral or philosophical themes. He also believed that the poet had to consciously put some "truth" into the poem or it would not have any. He
apparently could not believe that a poem might have a meaning
of which its author was not conscious or one that he had not intended. Wordsworth found creative activity valuable because it
helped him to bring forth something of worth, but he clearly
assigned a much lower order of importance to the delight or
enjoyment the work brought than to its moral or intellectual
content. He obviously did not feel that a personal poem could
have a meaning and a worth of its own. Nor did he believe that
what the poet reveals of himself is of interest to others; he was
perhaps unaware that other readers recognize their own condition through the poet's interpretation of his own personal experience.

The idea that autobiographical writing is "vain and frivolous" is very deeply rooted. Many writers whose work is autobiographical feel that they must justify it. They try to do so by
pointing out that through it readers can learn a great deal about
themselves. Proust's narrator remarks that art enables us to see
the world through another's eyes, giving us an understanding
and insight we could never otherwise have attained. Other writers have felt that their work could benefit others by sharing the
artist's special knowledge.

Montaigne, who as an essayist, was under less pressure to
justify himself than poets and novelists, nevertheless thought it
necessary to warn the readers of his *Essays* that they might be
wasting their time on a "vain and frivolous subject," because the
book was not written with any readers in mind other than a few
intimate friends and family members. Like Montaigne, many
artists feel that autobiographical material is inherently reprehen-
sible and fear that materials uniquely their own are not intrinsically worthwhile. Many have felt the need to say to the reader,
as Hugo did: "Don't you see that when speaking of myself, I am
also speaking about you."

Even Rousseau, who claimed to be unlike anyone else,
felt obliged to begin his *Confessions* by stating that he wanted his
readers to moan over the indignities he had suffered and to
blush in shame over the miseries he had endured. He was
implying, of course, that such feelings on his reader's part might
prevent other men from suffering what he had suffered; he also
appealed to their sense of justice. He remarked that his

confessions would be an example for others to follow. They too would bare their souls before God and thereby become conscious of their motivations. This would be invaluable as it would bring them greater self-knowledge and understanding. The *Confessions*, which at first appear to be an enterprise of self-glorification, are designed to make others aware of themselves, to make them conscious of what they would never have known had they not read this book. It is also possible that Rousseau was being hypocritical when he made these statements.

Wordsworth was very far from according individuality the importance that Rousseau did. Nor did he have Rousseau's conviction that the detailed analysis of his characters and the events of his life would enable other men to understand themselves better, and to question their customs, beliefs and role in society. Rousseau's manner (almost free association) and his desire to go far beyond the hypocritical conventions of his time, should have made a strong impact on men of the next generation. Yet Wordsworth said nothing about Rousseau's groundbreaking and liberating example. Quite possibly he was, by temperament and circumstances, better adjusted to his situation in life than was Rousseau. Wordsworth was too traditional to claim special attention for individuals with exceptional gifts. Though he lived in a time when some of the excesses of men of genius were tolerated, he was reluctant to claim special status—as if he were afraid of it—and thus did not publish *The Prelude*. He continued to hold a traditionalist view of the role of the artist, in a time when such a view was changing, perhaps more rapidly than ever before.

****

The formidable obstacles which Robert Musil encountered in writing his major unfinished novel, *The Man Without Qualities*, have been discussed by numerous critics. Musil's problems were caused by factors peculiar to his temperament and personality, and by his being caught up in the maelstrom of the second World War.

Musil's difficulties were in great part due to his financial circumstances and to his self-imposed exile, first from Germany, upon the establishment of the Third Reich, and then from Austria after the Anschluss. He moved to Switzerland in the summer of 1938 and died there four years later at the age of 62. He either lost his job as an engineer or gave up this profession in the 1920's hoping to be able to devote himself to his writing. Inflation soon exhausted his funds. He and his wife found themselves in the most trying of circumstances, often able to make ends meet only with enormous difficulty, usually by grace of last minute advances from Musil's publisher and gifts from a few admirers. At least two people who knew Musil personally have written that he was greatly depressed and demoralized by the lack of impact his work seemed to have had and by the silence, indifference and incomprehension with which it was received.[16]

As early as 1900 Musil had thought about what was to become his major novel, *The Man Without Qualities*. He began work on it in 1920 and the first part appeared in 1930. The second part was published in 1932 and the third part, edited by Musil's widow Martha, came out in Switzerland in 1943. Few people knew then that Musil had arranged for publication of the third part of his book in 1939 but had taken back the galley-proofs from the publisher, intending to revise them. He did not do so to his satisfaction and therefore this printing never took place. In 1952, *The Man Without Qualities* appeared in one volume edited by Adof Frisé, who had been able to consult all the papers left by Musil. This edition includes various fragments and numerous drafts of chapters found among Musil's papers.

After the publication of Adolf Frisé's edition of *The Man Without Qualities*, it became evident that Musil had written a huge number of drafts for chapters of his novel. The dating of these drafts, their possible use by their author in the "definitive" form of the novel and the order in which they would have been placed and used, if at all, cannot be determined with certainty. Scholars are working on these papers and hope, with the aid of computer programs, to determine through a study of themes at what point in the creation of the novel these various drafts were written.

Musil had begun to work on *The Man Without Qualities* in 1920 and it was clear to him in 1932, before his exile from Germany, that he would most likely not be able to finish his most ambitious work. After completing the second part of the novel, he wrote a "testament" or postface (1932). In it he stated that he did not know whether he would ever finish his book and thought he might have to interrupt it or abandon it before long.

He then gave reasons for believing that he would not finish the novel, but his reasons were confined to his financial problems.

Later in 1932, he wrote two other versions of this "testament." In the "testament II" he explained that, barring some unexpected development, he would not be able to finish the novel, and again alleged financial difficulties as his reason. But he went on to add some remarks concerning his method of working which explain his artistic difficulties in finishing his work. He states that his relationship to his subject was one of hesitation. He was juggling several subjects at the same time and retained them even after he was no longer enthusiastic about them, (and even if he had never been enthusiastic at all). He notes that he arbitrarily interchanged parts of his subject so that they travelled from one draft to another without his ever finding a definitive place for them. In the "Testament III" he explains that he viewed the sinking of his work, because of his inability to finish it, exactly in the same manner that he would view the sinking of a ship in mid-ocean. He again states that this disaster was the result of his precarious financial situation.

As Maurice Blanchot and Philippe Jaccottet have already pointed out, Musil's plan for *The Man Without Qualities*, a novel he worked on for over twenty years and whose project evolved in his mind for twenty years before that, changed greatly over this span of time.[17] These changes in the plan brought about interminable correcting, adding, deleting, revising and rewriting, but quite aside from this Musil was an inveterate believer in revision and rewriting for artistic reasons. In a 1928 interview, he stated that he reworked large parts of his work and even the whole of it up to twenty times.[18] In his notebooks he expressed the wish that the novel remain unpublished until he might cut and tighten the manuscript.[19] The fact that he had published parts of his novel before the whole was finished gave him the feeling that he was no longer free to complete it as he might wish. He was now bound by what he had written in the published segments.

The same notebook contains the statement that he was incapable of foreseeing the extension of a plan of any amplitude before actually beginning to write (*Tagebücher*, 449). His problem also stemmed from the impression of having in mind a swarm of possibilities; he felt like someone trying to wrap and tie a package larger than himself (*Tagebücher*, 329). A few lines before this statement, in the same notebook entry, he speaks of the difficulty of having many ideas at the same time and being unable to choose among them. Given the swarm of ideas and possibilities, any choice might be an impoverishment, a limitation or restriction for which he could find no justification. Musil's reluctance and inability to choose among a host of possibilities is one reason for his constant rewriting and the multiple drafts of chapters. Musil himself explains this inability to choose:

> It is while writing that what I believe is decided. Before, I think I believe many things; at the moment of expressing them, it becomes impossible to do so (*Tagebücher*, 450-451).

It appears from this statement that the act of writing itself paralyzed him so that he was able to express only a part of what he had thought before he took up his pen. We also have the impression that whatever Musil was finally able to express became what he believed, simply because he was able to put it down in writing. The things he couldn't find words for seemed afterwards to have vanished forever, unless they should somehow come back to haunt him. It appears that for every one thing he succeeded in putting down on paper, countless others floated in a limbo waiting for a later incarnation, so that later expressions might displace previous ones or might even coexist with them. They were just as valid but could not be set down earlier. Blanchot and Jaccottet both note that for Musil nothing was ever definitive, and things could always have been otherwise. Precisely for this reason, the swarm of ideas he carried in his head caused a ceaseless profusion of chapter reworkings.

The inability or unwillingness to choose between possibilities caused in Musil a kind of paralysis, which led him to say in a 1934 conversation with Martin Flinker that he could not see the end of his novel, that he was no longer master of it.[20] In view of the sketches, drafts, notes, remarks, postfaces and other materials he had accumulated during the composition of the book, this statement is quite understandable.

It appears from entries in the *Tagebücher* that one reason Musil had so much trouble selecting material from the numerous drafts he wrote and was unable to finish his novel was the same that prevented Paul Valéry from even beginning to write one. This was a sense of the arbitrariness of such an undertaking (*Tagebücher*, p. 485). The selection of details was most difficult for him as he thought details give a novel rigidity, a closure he found detrimental, as did many other novelists including Thomas Mann and Turgenev, both of whom Musil quoted on this subject.   Such closure or reductionism was all the more repugnant to him as his was a novel of ideas. He found it quite impossible to cut, to section off, and to limit, since the ideas led one to another, in a chain, though some links appear to be weaker than others. But the exploration of the various facets of these ideas is of the essence in a novel of this type. Precisely because of the kind of book he was writing, Musil could not follow the example of Celine, who told an interviewer that to end up with an 800 page novel it was necessary to write 80,000.[21]

In spite of his prolific output, Musil did have a "writing block," as innumerable entries in his diary attest. In it there are many expressions of his lack of faith in himself, his doubt about what he was writing and about the value of his art. He wrote at the end of September 1939 that he felt he was good for nothing and destined to achieve nothing of significance (*Tagebücher*, p. 470). Between 1937 and the end of 1941, he wrote that he often felt ready to give up writing and that he was a failure. He added that he had no confidence in himself but continued to drag himself to work. Every two or three days he felt, if only for a moment, that what he wrote was important (p. 480). He also stated that he should find a way of taking seriously, if not his work, then at least his intentions of days gone by (p. 478). He reproached himself for having always been too timid; he thought the "germ" of his "inhibitions" with regard to his work might be found in his timidity (p. 481). His self-criticism continues in this vein. He thought, for example, that it was a great mistake on his part to "stuff" too many ideas into *The Man Without Qualities*. He also realized that he didn't like many things he had written upon rereading his work, but did not want to change or modify it (p. 512). Although he made this statement with reference to one of his essays upon its publication, it is most likely that he had the same reaction when he wrote the many drafts of chapters of his novel and was unable to decide upon one "definitive" version.

In one page of his journal, Musil went into a fairly detailed explanation of how the "writing block" occurred. Upon revising the manuscript of volume I of *The Man Without Qualities*, he felt this paralysis but thought it normal when beginning the last revisions of a manuscript. When he began the revisions, he felt the need to rewrite the first chapter, and he had a satisfactory idea of how to proceed. He successfully completed the first part of the chapter but then the block occurred. When he worked on the continuation of the first part of his chapter, its form appeared awkward and he crossed out what had served as the middle of the chapter or transition. It occurred to him to insert at this point a passage he had not yet found a place for, a description of the sounds and rhythms of a large city. He saw approximately how this would lead into the third part of the chapter but his insight was still vague and fleeting. This he described as a classic situation: he had two solid pillars—the beginning and the end of the chapter—but could not find a transition to connect them. He inserted the descriptive passage but later deleted part of it.

He tried again to rewrite his original transition but became dissatisfied and realized that he had lost the general idea. He was unable to go on because of difficulties with stylistic details. The problems and the dissatisfaction he felt caused him to become so discouraged that he began to fear it would take him a year to complete his revisions of the manuscript. He noted that he had been hampered because he had not written down his ideas for the transition, but added that he would have been just as bothered if he had written them down.

The sense of blockage was like a physical sensation of pain. In a memorable page, Musil thought the best way to explain it was to call it "intellectual despair." This despair was a mixture of powerlessness combined with an extremely strong repugnance, as if he were afflicted with abulia. This recurred whenever his revisions seemed too daunting and he saw no way out of them. He stated that he had written this page on his sense of blockage so as to have his sentences before him, the better to manipulate them, as if by this means he could put his problem outside himself. He tried to exteriorize the problem to see if it then would not be more amenable to a solution than while it remained bottled up within himself (*Tagebücher*, pp. 301-302).

Musil's difficulty in mastering the enormous amount of detailed and complex material he had accumulated was in part due to the fact that *The Man Without Qualities* is not really a novel. As most critics have remarked, it "is not an attempt to tell a real story with a beginning and an end."[22]   As Jean-Francois Peyret points out, *The Man Without Qualities* is better described as a "montage."[23] He adds that the work is one of ideological criticism; Musil himself likened it to a Socratic dialogue.

This view goes a long way toward explaining why he could not finish the book. He was not working with such usually well determined elements as plot, character and description. By working within a genre, and accepting its conventions and traditions, novelists profit by using established patterns or configurations. They have an idea of what their characters must do, of the way they must live and of the manner in which situations must work themselves out once the *données* of a particular situation are established. This knowledge comes to the novelist because the characters begin, at some point, to assume a life of their own. The novel follows a logic inseparable from their personality and circumstances. The author cannot change these once the book acquires its independence.

A very famous example of this is a statement made by Proust in a July 1919 letter to a friend who had read the part of *Remembrance of Things Past* already published at that time. She had written to Proust to express her fears of experiencing much unhappiness in reading later parts of the novel, especially concerning Swann, whom she found a very likeable figure. The novelist answered that he himself was unhappy to see this character becoming less "sympathique" and even ridiculous, but added that he was not free to go against the truth or violate the laws of personality or character. He then added that he was a friend of Swann's but that above all he was a friend of Truth! He announced that, much to his chagrin, Swann would die as early as the fourth volume and would not be the main character of the book, although he, Proust, would have liked him to be just that. He ended the letter by stating that "art is a perpetual sacrifice of feeling to truth."

Musil also thought that his field was really philosophy and that he had not had the "courage" to be a thinker and philosopher. He introduced his ideas into his fiction where they were out of place and where it was, of course, impossible to do them justice. He added that he could certainly justify himself by saying that philosophy had not furnished him his ideas. Both philosophy and literature interested him equally—they were not clearly distinguishable in his mind. This made the writing of his novel all the more difficult. He was quite conscious that his novel was overwhelmed by the importance given to abstract ideas (*Tagebücher*, p. 458).

As Ernst Kaiser, Eithne Wilkins, Philippe Jaccottet and many others have pointed out, Musil's problem became more serious when he worked on the third part of his book after publishing the first and second parts which appeared in 1930 and 1932 respectively. In the third part of his novel he tried to describe life "in the Millenial Reign" ("ins tausendjahrige Reich") or what he called "the other state" ("der anderer zustand"). It is clear from reading the unfinished chapters left among Musil's papers (Nachlass) that in the last years of his life the novel had veered into a new and very different direction. It was in writing this new part that Musil experienced such difficulty. His problems were caused by his uncertainty concerning "the Millenial Reign" and "the other state," as he had much trouble in explaining their nature. From a reading of one of the most important completed chapters of the Nachlass—number 55—it appears that the protagonists are undecided or unable to choose between the active and the contemplative life, and seem to doubt that a viable synthesis of these can be achieved. The contemplative life, as the hero describes it, is itself a complex state; it has moments of ecstasy during which one lives at the highest point of one's possibilities, without any feeling of separation between consciousness and its objects. These states resemble Proust's privileged moments, and Musil too seems to have finally realized that it was impossible to create a work in which the characters would live a life made up of such epiphanies.

Most critics have stated that Musil was too much of a theoretician, essayist, analyst, thinker, satirist and empiricist to be the creator of a novel of mystical love. His corrosive irony prevented him from fully believing in "the Millenial Reign," or that his work alone mattered and was worth any and all sacrifices, however painful. The poet Philippe Jaccottet, who has translated much of Musil's work into French, notes that the novelist was torn apart by contradictions from childhood on. Musil was a rigorous, scientific thinker who prized logic and clarity above all. At the same time, he was a contemplative, valuing the life of the soul and the sensibility. This was a part of himself that his "logical" side viewed with aversion. Jaccottet believes that Musil never succeeded in reconciling these opposites and wore himself out trying. The "counterpoint" of this inner struggle explains the structure of *The Man Without Qualities*.[24] Flaubert experienced the same difficulties, but in his case the contradictions were not as stark and paralyzing. He also did not have the financial worries of his twentieth-century counterpart.

In a "curriculum vitae" he wrote in 1938, Musil noted

that, in *The Man Without Qualities*, "under the pretext of describing the last year of the Austrian Empire, essential questions concerning the existence of modern man are taken up."[25] These questions were to be answered in a totally new way. A friend of Musil's quoted him as saying that "a poet has a right to create only to the extent that he contributes to the spiritual betterment of the world."[26] Musil, like Wordsworth, had very high aims and a lofty idea of the function of literature. His satire of the country called Kakania, described in his novel, was undoubtedly intended to serve as a contrast to a better world whose reality would be the opposite of what was shown in the novel. But creating a new morality and contributing to the "spiritual betterment of the world" were forbiddingly difficult. Ulrich and Agatha, the protagonists of Musil's novel, find it hard to create a new order for themselves when it seems obvious that the world they live in is on the verge of total collapse. Even if Musil had been able to contribute a new morality for the betterment of mankind, it is unlikely that he would have had his characters live by it. In fact his view or morality was that it should not limit and restrain but rather help people to experiment ceaselessly with life, which should be "a choice among infinite numbers of possibilities."[27] A morality for all is useless and is even a contradiction in terms, as Musil believed precisely that each individual must choose or create his own. This is a belief he shared with those writers who, a few years after his death, would be called "existentialists."

One cannot discount the fact that Musil's doubts concerning his work were caused in part by what he felt to be the indifference with which it was received. He was painfully aware that in his time many lesser writers were far more successful than he knew he would ever be. But it is unclear why he could not see that these lesser writers appealed to a less demanding public, whom they supplied with much lighter and easier works than his. He certainly could not have written the books that brought success to other writers, even in the highly unlikely event that someone could have convinced him to do so. He simply was not an easy writer capable of attracting a wide public or of compromising his artistic standards and personal objectives. It is most unfortunate, as many people have noted, that his works were not translated into either English or French during his lifetime. This would have made his novel accessible to a much larger public and might have prompted foundations or patrons of the arts to grant him financial help, something that always eluded him when he was alive. Musil was not without contempt for a public which saved its applause for mediocre writers. He was disgusted by this situation and never spoke about the recognition posterity might give him. He did receive some recognition in his lifetime but not on a scale he found rewarding.

Spending all his time on his novel meant that for Musil the focus of his attention was narrowed to only one undertaking. In his case this may have been a mistake. He spent so much time writing different versions of his novel that he had no energy left for aesthetic decisions. It is also very hard to think of any satirist who has proposed something concrete to take the place of what he, the satirist, has destroyed or subjected to ridicule. When it comes to concrete proposals, satirists often sound impractical or utopian. Musil was less interested in projects to reform society than he was in exploring ways for individuals to effect changes in their manner of living.

The fact that he worked on the second part of his novel exclusively for ten years means that Musil must have lost some of his spontaneity, enthusiasm, and freshness of perspective, perhaps wondering if what he was doing was even possible. His own notion of what the second part of his novel should be like was too vague to allow him to find the form suitable to it. He tried out so many possibilities that in the welter of material he left, there is no indication that he had made any choice as to which ones were viable. His predicament was akin to that of Conrad, who wrote to his publisher in 1899: "You know how desperately slow I work: Scores of notions present themselves—expressions suggest themselves by the dozens, but the inward voice that decides—this is well—this is right—is not heard sometimes for days together."[28] Conrad, of course, heard the "inward voice" sooner or later. Musil did not, or not distinctly enough.

A contemporary French painter, André Masson, remarked that a great artist gives us a new conception of the rules of art, a new way of seeing the world or a new way of creating his work.[29] For the kind of novel he wanted to write, combining satire with a story of mystical love in an other-wordly realm, Musil needed one or all three of the elements described by Masson. The novel form could not accommodate a work such as he envisioned. He needed to change, modify, innovate and create one of his own just as his illustrious contemporaries Proust, Joyce and Kafka had done. The traditional novel format worked for the satirical part of his book but did not work for the second, more original part he had in mind. We will never know whether the originality of his concept of "the other state" could have taken form even if its creator had found an equally original manner of presenting his vision.

Musil remarked in his diary that his "timidity" was the "germ" of his inhibitions, his passivity and paralysis when facing his work. He asked himself what timidity was but did not answer his question (*Tagebücher*, p. 481). The very fact that he posed the question indicates some trepidation about what his art was revealing to him about himself as well as about others. He undoubtedly feared what he saw in his work, and wondered if it represented the truth or only some transient aberration. Musil was certainly not the first artist to stagger under the weight of self-knowledge. He wrote that his "irresolution" was the trait of his character that had tormented him most and the one he dreaded above all (*Tagebücher*, p. 482). His irresolution, of course, may have been the cause of his timidity. His writing, he said, had always lacked the "elan, the enthusiasm, the conviction of necessity" (*Tagebücher*, p. 485.) He felt that he had derived some advantages from this lack but did not go into details; he wondered if the time had not come to reach a "synthesis" (*Tagebücher*, p. 493).

Fear or hesitation in expressing his ideas as well as irresolution are the worst possible faults for an artist, who needs boldness, self-assurance, the desire to challenge, to criticize, to change things, to shock people out of their complacent routines. Musil noted that he was not a critic but an ironist. This sentence is itself a contradiction in terms. His irony was rather melancholy and not aggressive enough to galvanize his readers. It was too subtle to be understood by those who did not have the author's culture, intelligence and lucidity.

No one was more aware of the problems caused by his temperament and personality than Musil himself. He realized that his work could not attract the public's attention because he did not have the necessary eloquence and conviction. He was too "modest" and had an intelligence which ranged in too many opposite directions, one whose "ardor and violent passion" needed to be tempered by irony (*Tagebücher*, p. 499-500). He knew he was too serious and did not have the showmanship which seemed to come naturally to writers who were his contemporaries but, he felt, hardly his equals.

A stranger in an age that was somehow out of joint, deploring what he saw around him, Musil was not better prepared to find his way than were his protagonists Ulrich and Agatha. These young people found nothing to replace the values crumbling all around them. They were adrift in a world where the only salvation was their love for one another. They found nothing around them to replace the old order they saw decomposing before their eyes. It is clear from reading Musil's diaries that Ulrich's predicament was his creator's. Musil himself saw with lucidity that the world he had known was at an end, destroying itself with a barbarity he could not have imagined even though he had fought in the first World War and thought then that barbarity had reached its limits. The catastrophe could not be stopped in spite of all protests, petitions and attempts at political action which were too little and too late. Like Ulrich, Musil seemed paralyzed because his great perspicacity would not let him delude himself about the madness of the contemporary world. For all his passionate convictions, he could not transmit his beliefs to others, either because his convictions were not solid enough, because his feelings were numbed by the horror of what he saw, or because writers are more often witnesses than men of action.

Musil's hurt feelings and disappointment that his work was received with indifference are understandable, especially as *The Man Without Qualities*, which described the decline of Kakania (i.e. the Austro-hungarian Empire), was published at a time when the Western World was on the brink of the most destructive war ever. But to follow the story he told in the first two volumes with one of mystical love in an other-wordly realm would certainly have surprised the public. In the late nineteen thirties and early nineteen forties it is unimaginable that anyone in Europe could have shown much interest in such a story, except perhaps for its entertainment or escape value. This is certainly not what Musil wanted. His irresolution about how to continue the novel indicates that he may well have had doubts about the artistic merit of the projected conclusion because of the age he was living in. Had he stopped worrying about public acceptance and written about a utopia or millenial reign with the hope of being understood much later, he would have suffered far less anguish. That he could not conclude his novel along these lines shows that he considered his choice of "the Millenial Reign" a bad one either from the esthetic or the moral point of view, or from both.   If he could not finish *The Man Without Qualities* in the belief that the subject of a utopia in a time of cataclysm was tantamount to a massive sarcasm, then his inability to complete his novel becomes more readily comprehensible.

****

The sad distinction of having devoted a longer period of time to an unfinished work than any other artist belongs to the poet, short story writer, librettist, composer and critic Arrigo Boito (1842-1918).   In an article on Boito, William Ashbrook states that the list of the librettist's activities partly explains his problems.   One of these was that his limited talent ranged too widely in different fields.   He spent his energies wastefully, shuttling between music and literature.   Ashbrook notes that Boito's "uncertainty of purpose" hindered him from total concentration on any one project; this is clear from the artist's interrupted and unfinished endeavors.   Ashbrook also feels that Boito devoted more energy to advancing Verdi's career than his own.[30]   An earlier commentator, John Klein, noted that the librettist was overwhelmed by Verdi's activity and genius; disheartened by his own inferiority, Boito put his energies into writing librettos for the master.   The collaboration of the two men, ending with Verdi's death, did nothing to improve Boito's confidence in his capabilities.   In spite of Verdi's praise, Boito's association with the great composer brought him little confidence in his own talents.[31]

Radiana Pazmoor states that Boito spent so much time researching the background for his major work, the opera *Nerone*, that he got bogged down in period detail.   As a result, the work was adversely affected.[32]   She adds that the composer continued his research, piling up more and more details, until the end of his life.   He left his opera unfinished.   Giorgio Gualerzi writes that in Boito's case there was too wide a discrepancy between his knowledge and craft, (which were more than adequate), and his genius and inspiration insufficient to compose the kind of work that he aspired to create.[33]

Boito wrote, once to Verdi and once to a friend in France, that he suffered from a writer's block which prevented him from working at all. His creative activity had become a "night-mare." Unfortunately this was not a passing phenomenon. In the letter to Verdi he noted: "On days when I do not work, I accuse myself of idleness; on days when I do, I call myself an ass—and thus life runs by and I continue to exist, slowly suffocated by an ideal too high for me."[34] To his friend in France, the music critic Camille Bellaigue, Boito wrote that he suffered from "des crises d'agraphie," or moments when he was totally unable to write or compose. He added that he had had this complaint for over twenty-five years.[35] These crises of agraphia were most likely brought about by his frustration and inability to do what he expected to accomplish, because, as he had written to Verdi, he had undertaken a goal too high.

Boito could not abandon this ideal, yet never felt that his work brought him any closer to fulfilling it. He stuck with it, for not to do so would have diminished his self-regard and sense of purpose, as his letter to Verdi shows.

The sense of being unable to succeed in his undertakings and the resulting frustration are only visible in those cases where Boito worked on his own. When he collaborated with someone else he did not manifest any symptoms of a block. In his case, the Muse took the form of a two-faced creator in the sense that Boito only worked successfully when he could rely on the support he gained from collaboration with another artist, dead or alive. He had no trouble writing librettos on already existing works, as is evident from those he based on plays by Shakespeare (*Othello, Falstaff, Hamlet*), Victor Hugo (*Angelo, tyran de Padoue*) and Goethe (*Faust*).

In the last ten years of his life, Boito asked for the help of Arturo Toscanini, whose criticism of *Nerone* had distressed him. Upon Boito's death, the conductor explained in an interview that the score for this opera was written out only for voice and piano; the orchestration was not complete. Toscanini and the composer Tommasino proceeded to finish the orchestration following the detailed instructions left by the composer. Toscanini stated that Boito's problem was that instead of relying on what he felt, the librettist "swerved from his intuition and did not reach the effects that he foresaw and wished."[36]

The problems faced by Wordsworth, Boito and Musil are quite similar. These artists accumulated vast amounts of material which they could not shape into finished works despite long years of labor. In Boito's case this material consisted of roman history. In Musil's, the accumulation of notes gave rise to a proliferation of drafts of chapters that he might have included in his novel. Neither man was able to select, order and organize these materials into a completed work. Neither could decide on the material to be chosen and used for a number of reasons. Like Wordsworth, both felt that they had undertaken a work beyond their abilities. Rather than retrenching and setting less ambitious goals for themselves, they continued working and hoping, apparently against hope, that they might be able to compose the work they dreamed of. All three artists faced the problem mentioned by Joseph Conrad—not hearing the "inward voice" which tells the artist if what he is doing is good or not. That Boito "swerved from his intuition" is clear evidence that he did not hear that voice. This lack of self-confidence was also a factor in the inability of both Wordsworth and Musil to finish their works.

It may be that the creative instinct in these artists was not strong enough to surge through the barrier of self-consciousness. Perhaps in each man there was an unconscious or unadmitted refusal to allow elements from the deepest part of the inner self to come to the surface. But the intuitive impulses could not be completely repressed. The fact that so many years were spent on one work leaves little doubt that each artist kept trying to reconcile irreconcilable tendencies, those of consciousness versus those of intuitive instincts or impulses.

It is quite plausible to believe that these artists did not have a strong enough creative drive or motivation to begin with. Had they experienced a sense of urgency to express feelings of the utmost importance to them, had they been moved by a passion to express what they believed in or were totally committed to, they might not have wavered to such an extent. The motivating instinct seems not to have been felt with enough force to prompt them to work with the decisiveness needed.

It is also quite possible that our three artists were mistaken about the degree of their talent and capabilities. Perhaps they could not see that they had already done their best work and were pursuing a chimera. Boito wrote to Verdi: " . . . you live in the true, the genuine realm of art, and I in the world of hallucinations."37 It had occurred to Boito that he wasn't really working on anything of substance. But he also stated that even though he might not finish his opera, he would never abandon it. It was, after all, because they felt diminished at having nothing more to write that Hemingway, Montherlant, Romain Gary, John Berryman and Dylan Thomas committed suicide.[38]

Wordsworth, Musil and Boito continued to grapple with unfinished works because the struggle brought them some knowledge of what Proust called the "inner unknown homeland." The exploration of this unknown realm was of such importance that it was worth every effort, however unproductive and exhausting. These artists had a symbiotic relationship with their work which gave them a feeling of purpose, and it is probable that the compensations they drew from their work outweighed the anguish caused by their inability to complete it.

Notes

[1] Maurice Blanchot, "Proust," *Nouvelle Revue Française*, no. 20, août 1964, pp. 287-288.

[2] *Home at Grasmere: Part First, Book First, of The Recluse*, ed. Beth Darlington (Ithaca, N.Y., Cornell University Press, 1977), lines 686-691 and 697-702.

[3] Letter of May 21, 1807. *The Letters of William and Dorothy Wordsworth: The Middle Years, 1806-1811*, rev. Mary Moorman, 2nd ed. (Oxford: Clarendon, 1969), 146.

[4] Letter of April 29, 1804. *The Letters of William and Dorothy Wordsworth: The Early Years, 1787-1805*, rev. Chester L. Shaver, 2nd ed. (Oxford: Clarendon, 1967), 470.

[5] Letter of May 1, 1805, pp. 586-587.

[6] Detailed discussion of these problems can be found in Geoffrey Hartman, *Wordsworth's Poetry 1787-1814* (New Haven: Yale University Press, 1964), and M. H. Abrams, *Natural Supernaturalism: Tradition and Revolution in Romantic Literature* (New York: Norton, 1971).

[7] Letter of May 21, 1807, p. 147, see also *The Prelude*, XII, lines 208-335. All references to *The Prelude* are to the edition by Jonathan Wordsworth, M. H. Abrams and Stephen Gill (New York: Norton, 1979) and to the 1850 version, unless otherwise noted.

[8] A similar point was made by Carl Woodring, *Wordsworth* (New York: Houghton-Mifflin, 1965), p. 17.

[9] The resemblance between the "spots of time" passage and Proust's privileged moments was pointed out by M. H. Abrams in "*The Prelude* as the Portrait of an Artist," *Bicentenary Wordsworth Studies in Memory of John Finch* (Ithaca: Cornell University Press, 1970), pp. 180-237.

[10] *The Letters of William and Dorothy Wordsworth: The Later Years*, Part I, 1821-1828, rev. Alan G. Hill, 2nd ed. (Oxford: Clarendon, 1978), p. 50.

[11] Letter of December 17, 1831. *The Letters of William and Dorothy Wordsworth: The Later Years*, 1829-1834, rev. Alan G. Hill, 2nd ed. V, part 2 (Oxford, Clarendon, 1979), 464.

[12] Letter of March 6, 1804, p. 454. He repeated this statement in a letter of December 15, 1804, p. 518.

[13] *Coleridge on the Seventeenth Century*, ed. Roberta Florence Brinkley (New York: Greenwood Press Publishers, 1968), p. 578.

[14] Russell Noyes, *Wordsworth* (New York: Twayne, 1971), p. 155.

[15] See Beth Darlington, Preface to *Home at Grasmere* (Ithaca: Cornell University Press, 1977), p. 31.

[16] See Martin Flinker, "Mes Souvenirs de Robert Musil," and Otto Pacht, "A propos des oeuvres pré-posthumes," *Robert Musil, Cahiers de l'Herne*, ed. Marie-Louise Roth and Robert Olmi, No. 43 (1982), pp. 277-281 and 276-277.

[17] Maurice Blanchot, "Robert Musil," *Nouvelle Revue Française*, février 1958, pp. 301-309; mars 1958, pp. 479-490. Philippe Jaccottet wrote an important afterword to his translation of *L'Homme sans qualités* published in Paris by Editions du Seuil, 1979, and an introduction to his translation of Musil's diary: *Journaux de Robert Musil*, 2 vols. Editions du Seuil, 1981.

[18] Robert Musil, *Gesammelte Werke*, 3 vols. (Hamburg: Rowohlt, 1952-1957), II, 1978, 945-947.

[19] Robert Musil, *Tagebücher, Aphorismen, Essays und Reden* (Hamburg: Rowohlt, 1955), p. 451.

[20] Flinker, "Mes Souvenirs de Robert Musil," p. 279.

[21] See *Writers at Work*, second series (New York: The Viking Press, 1963), p. 86.

[22] David Luft, *Robert Musil and the Crisis of European Culture*, 1880-1942 (Berkeley: University of California Press, 1980), p. 216.

[23] Jean-Francois Peyret, "Musil ou les contradictions de la modernité," *Critique*, no. 339-340, août-septembre 1975, p. 862.

[24] Philippe Jaccottet, "Robert Musil," *Encyclopaedia Universalis*, 1985, Vol. XI, 476.

[25] Robert Musil, *Gesammlete Werke* II, 950.

[26] Martin Flinker, p. 278.

[27] *The Man Without Qualities*, II, chapter 38.

[28] Joseph Conrad, *Letters to William Blackwood and David S. Meldrum*, ed. William Blackburn (Durham, N.C.: Duke University Press, 1958), p. 64.

[29] André Masson, *Ecrits* (Paris: Hermann, 1976), p. 127.

[30] William Ashbrook, "The Two Faces of Boito," *Opera News*, April 10, 1976, p. 13. This critic also wrote an article on Boito in *The New Grove Dictionary of Music and Musicians*, ed. Stanley Sadie (New York: MacMillan, 1980), II, 863-867.

[31] John Klein, "The Enigma of Boito," *Opera*, March 7, 1968, pp. 191-197.

[32] Radiana Pazmoor, "The Librettists," *National Association of Teachers of Singing Bulletin* (NATS), February-March 1974, p. 21.

[33] "Nerone," *Opera*, November 26, 1975, pp. 1065-1066.

[34] Quoted by Michael Rose, "The Birth of an Opera," *About the House*, vol. 5, no. 5, Spring 1978, p. 61.

[35] *Revue des deux mondes*, 15 aout 1918, p. 901.

[36] Toscanini's remarks are quoted by Susan Backus in her excellent article "Boito's Unfinishable *Nerone*," *The Opera Journal*, XIV, no. 3, 1981, p. 24.

[37] Quoted by Michael Rose, p. 61.

[38] See Roger Asselineau, "Ernest Hemingway," *Encyclopaedia Universalis* (Paris: Encyclopaedia Universalis, 1985) IX, 194. On Berryman and Dylan Thomas see Eileen Simpson, *Poets in their Youth* (New York: Random House, 1982), pp. 239 and 253.

Disappointment, Despair and Destruction:

It has long been known that many artists set insurmountable problems for themselves. If the artist feels he cannot overcome them he has no way out but to redo the work, destroy it, or
set it aside, perhaps with the idea of working on it at a later time.
Many who find or create enormous difficulties in their path, believe that their work is far more important than their personal
happiness. If they do not destroy their creations, they go to
incredible lengths to work and rework them, ready to sacrifice
everything else in their life. Thus Balzac wrote to his future
wife that his novel *Seraphita* was crushing and killing him, and
that he was putting his whole life into it; there are many other
sentences to the same effect in his correspondence.[1]

In one of Henry James' most famous stories, "The Lesson
of the Master," a noted older writer persuades a younger one to
give up the idea of marrying the woman he loves, since a wife
and family can only waste an artist's time and energy and prevent him from accomplishing what he has envisioned. The
younger artist, believing that his older colleague did not fulfill
his potential because he is burdened with a wife and family,
accepts his advice with relatively little doubt as to its soundness.
Real as well as fictional artists make these sacrifices because they
believe art to have a higher value than any other
endeavor—only by virtue of his uniqueness and individuality
can the artist create a work of art. Many artists thus believe that
they have a creative mission. This sense of a calling can lead
artists to suffer martyrdom exactly as it leads others to sacrifice
their lives for a religious or ideological belief.

It does sometimes happen that an artist will question the
sense of his sacrifice. This was the case with Flaubert, who was
willing to live the life of a virtual recluse for his art. He noted
that others had already said all that he could hope to as well if
not better (*Corr.* I, 426). He could not always find a justification
for being an artist or for the way of life he had chosen. This lack
of a sense of mission did not cause him undue anguish, probably

because he suffered for other reasons, fearful as he was of not producing the very best writing he was capable of. He noted that he could hear the desired effects in his head but found it impossibly difficult to transcribe their sound (*Corr.* II, 440).

Like Flaubert before him, Kafka believed that total devotion to his art was the only justification for his life. He wrote to his fiancee of a "desire to torment myself for some higher purpose," although this "higher purpose" remained undefined.[2] He acted as if he believed in his mission quite completely and no amount of hardship would deflect him from his self-imposed goal. He also wrote in this same letter of his "fear of achieving happiness," but did not go into the causes of this fear. Happiness would presumably interfere with his goal and might lessen his resolve to do nothing but write. This "fear of happiness" can, of course, be attributed to many different reasons—feelings of unworthiness and guilt, a need for self-punishment, the belief that his life would be absurd if not devoted to his art, and a secular equivalent to what in religion is a commitment to a life of chastity, poverty and prayer. (The *Letters to Felice* show that the need for asceticism was very strong in Kafka). A list of such reasons could be endless and any attentive reader of his letters and diaries could find others, all valid to some degree. Yet although he felt that his art was his life, he did not really like any of his works:

> Can you understand this, dearest: to write badly yet feel compelled to write, or abandon oneself to total despair! . . . to see the pages being covered endlessly with things one hates, that fill one with loathing, or at any rate with such indifference, that nevertheless have to be written down in order that one shall live. Disgusting! If only I could destroy the pages I have written in the last four days, as though they had never been (*Letters to Felice*, p. 76).

Kafka in fact directed his friend and literary executor, Max Brod, to destroy all his unpublished works, letters, diaries, notes and papers after his death and have nothing reprinted. He not only talked of destroying his work but actually had his companion, Dora Dymant, burn twenty notebooks as he watched from his sickbed during the last year of his life.[3] In the "Postscript" to the first edition of *The Trial*, Max Brod related that when he went through his friend's papers, he found four thick notebooks of which all the inside pages had been burned; only the covers remained. Brod added that he knew from a reliable source, undoubtedly Dora Dymant, that Kafka burned or had someone burn several stacks of papers. Miss Dymant, in a memoir published in 1949 in *Der Monat*, stated that she "burned some of Kafka's works" evidently after his death and upon his specific instructions.[4]

In his correspondence Kafka mentioned having burned letters. He himself gave away the manuscripts of his diaries to his friend Milena Jesenska-Polak (*Diaries* II, 193). As Maurice Blanchot has noted, Kafka's diaries for the year 1923 are missing, having perhaps been burned as part of the twenty notebooks or of other stacks of papers.[5] It is not known whether Kafka kept a diary for the early part of 1924, when he still had strength to write. As for the writings of his youth, some pieces he wrote in 1903, 1904-1905 and 1907-1908 have disappeared.[6]

In a letter to Felice dated March 9-10, 1913, Kafka noted that for his novel *Amerika*, he had written a total of five hundred fifty pages which he considered worthless; these pages he presumably destroyed. His dissatisfaction came from the fact that most of what he had written was "from recollection of deep but totally absent feelings and consequently has to be rejected" (p. 218). If dissatisfied with the strength and intensity of his feelings while writing, he considered the product flawed and deserving only to be destroyed. For him there could be no question of "emotion recollected in tranquillity;" only while under the spell of intense feelings did he feel that he could produce forceful and accurate prose. This is the main reason why he liked to complete a story in one sitting even if it took all night.

Kafka had other reasons for wishing to destroy his work. One was directly connected with what he considered to be the responsibility of the artist. He was afraid of going too far, of harming others with the truth of what he saw. He told Gustav Janouch:

> One must be silent if you can't give help. No one through his own lack of hope should make the condition of the patient worse. For that reason, all my scribbling is to be destroyed. I am no light, I have lost my way among my own thorns. I'm a dead end.[7]

He thought that much of what he had written was not the truth but a view of life colored by his particular subjective outlook or by his illness: perhaps what he had expressed was a distortion caused by his personal circumstances. He was well aware that he often expressed things without understanding them fully and thought this another reason for not tormenting others with his interpretations, whose validity even he was uncertain of. He was not always able to explain to himself the import of what he had written. In a letter to his fiancee, he asked if she could see "any straightforward, coherent meaning" in his story "The Judgment or "explain anything in it" (p. 265).

In a letter to Max Brod, written at the end of October 1923, Kafka notes that a work of art is justified if it makes possible "the exchange of truthful words from person to person."[8] But he evidently had qualms as to whether artists should always express the truth, if it causes harm to do so. However, even when the artist did know the truth, Kafka believed that setting it down in all its subtlety and detail was almost impossible, simply because artists are rarely capable of doing so.

As for himself, Kafka claimed that his prose was too imprecise to effectively transcribe his emotions (*Diaries* I, 152). Like many other artists he was often dissatisfied with his own work which, conceived in a moment of inspiration, became "dry, wrong, inflexible . . . patchy" in the writing, even though he "had forgotten nothing of the original conception" (*Diaries* I, 151).

Kafka had a most ambivalent attitude toward his art. He considered it to be the sole means of salvation available to him, his only hope of achieving some inner peace. He described his inner life as the war of two forces he could not control, one good, the other evil. From time to time these forces reversed their roles and this only added "confusion" to the situation.[9] He gave the impression that he was the helpless spectator to an incomprehensible struggle.

Most of the letters and diary entries from the last four or five years of Kafka's life show his ambivalence toward writing. He had always, until 1921, insisted that writing was his whole life, that he *was* his novels and stories, that he cared little for anything beside this need or mission to write.[10] The change of belief evident in the last years could be attributed to the physical suffering, insomnia, and moments of depression caused by his illness, although he had had these symptoms prior to the onset of the tuberculosis of which he was to die. But the effects of this worsening illness caused Kafka to reassess his past life and most of the beliefs he had held until his already poor health deteriorated further. Max Brod noted, in the Postscript to the first edi-

671 86249

tion of *The Trial*, that around 1921 Kafka's autocritical tendencies had reached their highest point.

This reassessment of his beliefs is visible in a letter to Brod dated July 5, 1922, two years before Kafka's death. This letter and other writings of this period show, for the first time in such direct fashion, that his art was almost a torture for Kafka and drained him of his remaining strength. It appeared to him now to have prevented him from living and to have led him to the pursuit of chimeras. This was a complete change of attitude on his part as, on at least two occasions, he had noted that he would like to shut himself up like a hermit, wall himself off as in a tomb where he would do nothing but write (*Letters to Felice*, pp. 156, 279). In 1913 (June 10-16), he had also written to his fiancee that he felt he had, at an "almost inaccessible depth," certain creative powers. But he was reluctant to commit himself to them; he felt the need to do so but heeded his "inner warnings." Yet he felt that going to these depths in order to create would "lift me out of my inner misery in an instant" (*Letters to Felice*, p. 270). In 1922, it appeared to him that a writer's descent to the depths of consciousness or to the unconscious was a mad, dangerous activity which "unleashed spiritual forces" it was better to restrain. The writer cannot control these forces and in their presence he is like the sorcerer's apprentice. Such writing, based on contact with the depth of consciousness, only prolongs the artist's "narcissim." If this be the case, any knowledge gained by this degree of introspection is bad and threatening.

Kafka's unhappiness concerning such writing led him, rightly or wrongly, to pass some very harsh judgments upon himself. He stated in the letter to Brod: "I have remained clay, I have not fanned the spark of life to a flame but simply used it to illuminate my own corpse."[11] Such a sentence, from a writer who claimed all his life to *be* literature and nothing else, is an admission of failure, of having lost his way and wasted his life. He added that he now felt that writing depended "on the ability to forget oneself." Convinced that he had not been able to do so, he spoke of the necessity of "abjuring narcissism." The word Kafka used was "selbstgenuss" which literally means "enjoyment of oneself." He accused himself of having produced writing which was "vanity and hedonism." In retrospect, he felt that he had lived without any solid basis, and had been the plaything of an unknowable power emerging from a dark void presumably within him. These statements confirm, once again, his sense of being the battleground of forces he could not control, forces which were tearing him apart.

Although rarer prior to 1921, statements showing Kafka's awareness of the destructive power of writing had long been evident in his letters and diaries. In June 1913, he noted in his *Diary* that he carried in his head a world from which he could not free himself without being torn asunder. He thought it better to be torn apart than to supress what he experienced. In fact he was certain that his mission in life was to express the world he carried within him (*Diaries* I, 288). The tug of war between conflicting needs probably best explains his desire to destroy his work, the product and reflection of an unfulfilled, unlived life. He noted in 1920 that his writing was a mandate which nobody had given him and that it was only on this unsought mission, "always only on a contradiction, that I can live."[12] In April 1921 he had written to Brod that he only loved what he could place so high above himself that it became unattainable.[13] As the July 5, 1922 letter to Brod shows, Kafka did not find in art the value which would justify the single-mindedness with which he approached it, the sacrifices he had made on its behalf. He now regretted these, saying of himself (and his kind): "He dies (or does not live) and always feels sorry for himself" (Letter of July 5, 1922).

At this moment in his life he could not find enough satisfaction in his work to compensate for what he had given up. He had become an artist who expected his creation to give him a value, a fulfillment as well a feeling of its intrinsic worth. When it did not, he blamed it and himself for being unworthy. He felt drained, lost, resentful and ready to condemn writing as a narcissistic activity, as "vanity" and "devil-worship." In October 1921, he wrote in his diary that he had systematically destroyed himself in the course of the years, a sad verdict if true (*Diaries* II, 195).

Many artists have felt that what they created could be of use to others, that they had expressed what all men felt at one time or another and in this sense had spoken for humanity. Some, like Flaubert, Proust, Martin du Gard, Wordsworth, believed that through their description of their personal experience, others would benefit by gaining an understanding of their own situation. But Kafka worried that his condition was so unique, and his experience so peculiar and unusual, that his writing could only harm his readers.

Until about 1922 Kafka acted as if his art were a means of establishing a relationship or bridge between the selves within him. He needed to find in his work a means of exorcising his inner struggle. But it appears that his writing did not bring him what he sought. According to the companion of his last year, Dora Dymant, "there were times when he wanted to burn everything he had written, in order to free his soul from these ghosts." These, according to her, included "everything that had tormented him prior to his arrival in Berlin."[14] She added that in Berlin "he had freed himself from the tyranny of the past." But if this had really been the case, would Kafka have demanded that his notebooks be thrown into the fire while he watched them burn from his bed? It is, of course, possible that he did feel free of the burdens of his past and ordered the destruction of the notebooks and papers so as not to leave behind what he considered no longer important to him. Such writings might only mislead others and cause them to despair of man's moral plight. One hopes that the statements by Dora Dymant are true. If so, they indicate that Kafka had finally overcome his need to create insurmountable obstacles for himself. Perhaps, as in so many other cases, Kafka wanted to destroy what he considered mediocre work.

When artists destroy their creations they often make serious errors in judgment. They deprive readers of books that might have been of the highest interest and might eventually have led them to greater understanding of the artist and of themselves. Kafka's belief in the utter singularity of his experience, of its strangeness and the deleterious effects it might have on others is most unusual. It is particularly ironic in view of the fact that so many of Kafka's readers have judged him to have given a perfect representation of twentieth century man, a representation to be found in no other writer.

****

The composer Paul Dukas (1865-1935) abandoned numerous projects and destroyed his works on a massive scale. G. W. Hopkins lists fifteen published works by this composer and eleven either abandoned or destroyed.[15] Dukas' letters give virtually no information concerning these compositions. Our only knowledge concerning them comes from a very few of his friends whose articles appeared in a special number of *La Revue Musicale* (mai-juin 1936) as a hommage to the composer. Even to these friends Dukas confided little or none of his fears, hopes and disappointments and was always extremely reluctant to speak of himself and his work. His correspondence contains only two letters which shed some light on his difficulties as a creative artist.

The first letter, dated 1893, when he was 28, was addressed to a former teacher, the composer Vincent d'Indy. Already in 1893, Dukas spoke of the factors causing a "paralysis" of his inspiration. He wrote that he experienced great perplexities and fears in his creative work; he spoke of it as a torture. He felt that in compensation for the agonies he underwent there were tremors ("secousses") or exceptional moments when everything seemed easy. But he added that these moments were rare and could only be brought on by the accumulation, and then expenditure, of a great amount of what he called "vital fluid." These words remind one of Freud's libido, also limited in quantity, and of Balzac's theory about the limited amount of creative energy any artist has at his disposal. Dukas added that this "vital fluid" was not always available and that the spending of creative energy was followed by sadness and depression.

In exceptional moments of inspiration, Dukas glimpsed extraordinary ideas which transported him to another realm. Unfortunately, these ideas could not be grasped or held, as they were too volatile. They were a challenge to the artist, and he noted that in effect they were the source of works he would find it impossibly difficult to create. He thought it was even too dangerous to live with these ideas, which only produced disdain towards the less "exquisite" of his works which, nevertheless, came so much more easily to him.

Dukas felt he had been wrong to live so long with these "chimeras" of inspiration in his head and added that they caused artists to be too demanding and unjust with themselves. He thought these "monsters" of the artist's dreams would devour him if he did not suppress them. The very struggle against these chimerical ideas could make him strong, teaching self-control and mastery over them. Inspiration was for Dukas a fearsome and paralyzing rather than productive experience. He did not say that inspiration came to him in a flash, but rather that he had to bring it about through the accumulation and expenditure of vital energies. He stopped just short of saying that these energies should be channelled directly toward the production of work, apparently because this could not be done. Instead the accumulation of vital energy produced tremors, or moments of exaltation, which led to nothing. Such moments gave him the sensation of being transported outside himself on a surge of freedom and limitless creative power. But once they passed, he felt disappointed and depressed. He could not even grasp the ideas he had glimpsed, much less use them. By contrast with what he had seen in these moments of exaltation, the work he could do when not so inspired appeared dull and not worthwhile.

In his article, G. W. Hopkins suggests that Dukas' silence between 1912 and 1920, and his dissatisfaction with his work, can be attributed to the likelihood that "he had ceased to experience a sense of creative excitement such as would have sustained his more youthful work: he had perhaps become too much the master of his craft, having set himself, and met, great challenges but lost his relish for fresh discoveries."[16] This explanation is very plausible, but the 1893 letter to d'Indy indicates quite clearly that the composer could no longer continue on the path he had followed until then. He himself had stated in that letter that he equated inspiration with "chimeras" and could not afford the mental or emotional toll of inspired creation. But it is quite true that Dukas could have "ceased to experience a sense of creative excitement," which is not, after all, the inspired rapture that he had described in 1893.

In a letter of 1925, he wrote that he thought he was a composer again after many years of silence. Two compositions, *La plainte, au loin, du faune* and *Sonnet de Ronsard* appeared in 1920 and 1924 respectively. Judging from his statements in this letter, the aforementioned works were composed under the protection of a less tyrannical Muse, with the composer's "inspiration" being less tormented and feverish. He wrote that after many flirtations with others, the Muse had turned her attentions toward him again—a man less brilliant, older, but more trustworthy, in whom she could have greater confidence.[17]

These few lines, in the nature of a joke, nevertheless indicate that Dukas was torn between contradictory feelings he could not reconcile. He thought he could not successfully give form to what he had experienced in moments of exaltation, at a tremendous cost of psychic and nervous energy and strain. This instability left him feeling both his inferiority and the folly of undertaking what he could not hope to accomplish. He loved his art beyond anything and had an extremely exalted notion of it; he wrote that the mission of true art was to produce truth in a world of false art and lies.

If Dukas abandoned and/or destroyed eleven finished or nearly finished works, it is natural to assume that despite his mastery, the composer believed he had been defeated in the impossible struggle to accomplish what he could not.[18] In his struggle against the "chimeras," or moments of inspiration, he had perhaps found the strength to overcome them and was happy that he had done so, but did not feel that his later work was good enough.

Dukas apparently abandoned and destroyed works belonging to all periods of his creative life. G. W. Hopkins lists among such works seven dating from 1883 to 1912. Three are undated and one was composed in 1930. It appears from the testimony of Dukas' friends that he rarely consulted anyone before he destroyed his works. Georges Favre stated that one of them, *La Peri* (1911) was saved from destruction only after he uncharacteristically asked for advice from friends, including his former teacher Vincent d'Indy.[19]

From remarks made by his friends, it is clear that Dukas was a withdrawn individual, secretive about his work, and disinclined to discuss his problems with anyone. Most of his friends mention his anxiety, his uncertainties, his lack of confidence, his scruples, and his self-criticism. There was no doubt in the mind of at least one of them, the conductor Robert Brussel, that the works destroyed by the composer were of great beauty. Brussel had apparently seen these pieces and could not understand why they had been sacrificed. He believed that those who claimed that acts of destruction were motivated by a "destructive sense of criticism of the creative function" were adopting a "simplistic" explanation.[20]

Dukas rarely sought the encouragement or support of devoted friends, either because of deep reticence, or self-doubt, or a fear that his friends would not give him an objective opinion. He may have feared that they would be unwilling to be frank; perhaps he deemed them unqualified to make a critically valid judgment. Yet many were composers and conductors. It may well be that he refused to admit to himself that he needed their encouragement.

It cannot be merely a coincidence that Dukas' most popular work is entitled *The Sorcerer's Apprentice*. The apprentice of the legend knew only one half of a magic formula, allowing him to initiate awesome processes but not to control them. The waters he caused to rise did so until they threatened to engulf him; he was saved only by his master's last-minute arrival. It may be that Dukas felt himself to be in the same situation as the sorcerer's apprentice, as he could not control the awesome creative powers he had glimpsed within himself. He may have sensed that by giving free rein to his imagination he would produce so much as to be engulfed by his run-away production. He would then not even have the force of will to stop it. Perhaps he was of the opinion that a work of art may acquire a momentum and independence of its own; its creator may thus lose some measure of control over it. The artist, like the sorcerer's apprentice, does not always realize exactly what forces he unleashes and may not know how and why he does so. He may be overwhelmed by his own creation, which can become a monstrous thing, threatening and even destroying its creator. The apprehension of creative inspiration betrayed in Dukas' letter to d'Indy permits such a hypothesis to be entertained quite seriously.

The possibility of Dukas' being carried away by his vision is suggested by a key statement: "Within myself, I join an anarchic temperament to the inheritance of a punctual and meticulous conscience."[21] Such a division of inner forces can only hinder an artist, and may impel one as modest yet as exigent as Dukas to destroy his work. He could not reconcile the two antagonistic poles of his temperament, the Dionysian and Apollonian, the romantic and classic, the passionately untamed and the precisely disciplined. But the possibility cannot be excluded that the works he destroyed deserved to be published. He may have burned them because he felt they showed traces of his own inner conflicts and of his inability to overcome them.

Dukas had a temperament very similar to Flaubert's. The novelist managed to reconcile the antagonistic drives within himself, or at least to control them. Dukas' destruction of his works does not necessarily mean that he could not have done the same. It may be that he was simply less successful in overcoming his doubts and anxieties about himself.

****

Georges Rouault (1871-1958) destroyed three hundred fifteen of his canvases under very unusual circumstances. The act
was the result of a combination of factors which explains a great
deal about the painter's life and working methods.

In 1913, quite poor, married, with a family, having sold
virtually nothing until the age of forty—his style of painting was
very unpopular at the time,—Rouault sold the entire contents of
his workshop to the dealer Ambroise Vollard.[22] The contents of
the workshop included seven hundred seventy paintings (mostly unfinished), watercolors and drawings, which Vollard bought
for forty-nine thousand francs. The painter objected to selling so
many unfinished works, but Vollard's policy was to buy everything an artist produced, or nothing. According to Maurice
Coutot, who was later Rouault's attorney, the dealer told the artist that he would have the rest of his life to finish the un-
completed works. The painter's daughter, Geneviève Nouaille-
Rouault, states that her father agreed to finish the paintings
Vollard had purchased.[23]

Due to the war, the terms of the sale were not effected
until 1917, when Vollard became Rouault's dealer with exclu-
sive rights to his work. He put at the painter's disposal a studio
located first on rue de Grammont and then on rue de Martignac,
in the very building where he himself lived. This prompted
critics to say that the dealer had bought not only the paintings
but the painter as well. Pierre Courthion, the art historian and
critic, wrote that the agreement between dealer and painter
included the proviso that Rouault was to be consulted before-
hand whenever the dealer sold one of the unfinished paintings.[24] It appears that this arrangement worked more or less to
the satisfaction of both parties. Courthion noted that Vollard
never pressured Rouault to turn over canvases he was not ready
to release for sale (p. 295). But Georges Chabot and Maurice
Coutot say that Vollard put pressure on the painter to turn over
canvases to him, and made him a "work-horse."[25] Others assert
that it was Vollard who used the phrase "work-horse" ("un
bourreau de travail") a propos of Rouault.[26] More recently, François Chapon has indicated that over the long years of their association, Vollard showed a "mercantile mistrust" of Rouault's
ardor in the pursuit of perfection and a "plaguing pettiness."[27]

In addition to the agreement involving the paintings, watercolors, and drawings, Vollard, who published expensive, limited-edition, illustrated art books, kept Rouault very busy. He commissioned the artist to do a large number of prints, etchings, lithographs, wood-cuts and copper plate engravings for these art books. Rouault threw himself into this work with his customary zeal for perfection and sometimes did up to fifteen plates before he found one to be satisfactory.[28] In twenty-four years, Rouault turned over to Vollard one hundred sixty-four such engravings, in addition to two hundred sixty-six drawings for wood-cuts and one hundred sixty-two etchings.

In 1939, Vollard died in a car accident, but shortly before his death he had entered into a new written contract with Rouault. At the time of this agreement, Vollard owned five hundred thirty nine finished paintings and eight hundred nineteen unfinished ones which Rouault promised to complete by the terms of the contract. After the dealer's death his heirs divided all the works among themselves, the finished as well as the unfinished ones. The painter feared that they would sell the unfinished works as they were, because by 1938 anything by Rouault was worth a lot of money. Growing more and more anxious about this, he finally decided to sue Vollard's heirs to recover possession of the unfinished paintings, a suit apparently initiated in 1943.[29] In 1947, the court ruled that Rouault was indeed the legal owner of everything he had left unfinished and was to have the last word on how the works were to be disposed of. Rouault returned to Vollard's heirs the advance payment he had received for these works and they turned over to him seven hundred nineteen unfinished items.

Since there had been eight hundred nineteen works in Vollard's possession in 1938, it is clear that the heirs retained one hundred paintings in defiance of the court order.[30] Of the seven hundred fifteen paintings returned to him, Rouault had three hundred fifteen burned in a factory furnace in his presence with a court official, a photographer and a cameraman as witnesses (1948).

Rouault's daughter, Isabelle, told Pierre Courthion that her father ordered destroyed only those works he felt he could not finish in his lifetime. According to her, the only consideration in her father's mind was "the stage of progress of each painting" and he had burned "only those works which he felt so little advanced that completion would demand too long a time."[31]

This statement by his daughter brings up the question of Rouault's methods of working. Back in 1926, the critic Georges Charensol described the painter's work habits in a book entitled *Rouault, l'homme et l'oeuvre.* He usually started a canvas, then put it aside for months at a time, did some work on it and then put it aside again, sometimes finishing a work many years after having begun it. Charensol explained that Rouault had not had an exhibit in about twelve years (the last one had taken place in 1917), although he had not stopped painting, and that most of his work consisted of sketches. He went on to say that many of Rouault's works on the market were sketches too, and yet sold at very high prices as if they were finished works. It appears, therefore, that unfinished works by Rouault were on the market and not only in Vollard's store rooms.

In view of his work habits, it is hard to believe that the painter was unrealistic enough to think that he could eventually get around to finishing all the canvases he had turned over to Vollard. He was himself quite conscious of his own character and in 1913 had written to his friend, the poet André Suarès, that he was never satisfied with himself and was always conscious of progress to be made.[32] Charensol's description of Rouault's working habits is probably the first but by no means the only one, and his account is reliable. It is confirmed by Bernard Dorival, who noted in 1964 in the catalogue to the exhibit of Rouault's unfinished works (given to the Louvre in 1961 by Rouault's wife) that the painter nearly always began a work with a spontaneous outpouring. He also spoke of the "immediately translated impetuosity of this veritable creative eruption."[33] But once this had taken place, the painter worked and reworked his canvases endlessly, with patience and tenacity, as long as he felt it necessary to do so. In November 1948, at the time Rouault had the three hundred fifteen unfinished canvases burned, the critic for *Time* magazine noted:

> Rouault has a habit of keeping his paintings locked up in his studio for years on end, signing them only when he is sure he cannot improve them by so much as a single stroke of the brush (November 15, 1948).

Since Rouault was constitutionally unable to admit that one of his works could not be improved by reworking it, he felt a need to hold on to all of them as long as possible and parted with them only with the utmost reluctance and anxiety. In this behavior he was not alone; other painters with a similar mania include Turner, Degas, Bonnard and Soutine.   In view of Rouault's attitude it is a wonder that of the seven hundred fifteen canvases returned to him he only destroyed three hundred fifteen.   Even though he was seventy eight in 1948, he must have believed that he had enough strength to complete most of the remaining four hundred-odd works.   In a review of the 1964 exhibit of the unfinished works given to the Louvre, Pierre Courthion states that the painter was so conscientious that "he considered unfinished paintings to which he had not given the sign of their completion: his signature."[34]

From this remark and others in the article, it is clear that Courthion felt most items in this exhibit could be considered finished; only Rouault's high standards stopped him from signing them.   The same point was made by Georges Charensol and by Claude Roger-Marx.[35]   Rouault had made a habit of not signing his work in order to be free to return to it and change it more easily.   According to Jacques Lassaigne, this habit began in 1937, but Courthion claimed that it dated back to 1922.[36]   It is not possible to know how many paintings Rouault worked on or completed between the time he recovered them from Vollard's heirs (1948) and his death (1958), because he did not let members of his family into his studio.   He even refused to show his paintings to his best friends.[37]

It is quite clear that Rouault could not finish his works because he undertook too many; the sheer numbers proved too much for him.   Another factor was his reluctance to concede that he could no longer add anything to a work or modify it in any way.   His failure to sign many apparently finished paintings is one indication of this.   For many artists the problem is just as difficult as it was for Rouault.   The painter Philip Guston (1913-1980) wrote:

> For me the most relevant question and perhaps the only one is, "When are you finished? When do you stop? Or rather why stop at all? But you have to rest somewhere. (*Art News Annual*, p. 103).

Precisely because there is such difficulty in deciding where to stop, artists, as Guston indicated, begin to believe that whatever decision they finally make is arbitrary and might as well have been taken either earlier or later.   In the same paragraph Guston goes on to state that "unless painting proves its right to exist by being critical and self-judging, it has no right to exist at all—or is even possible."

As these lines show, some artists are disturbed by the fact that their decision to end a work is, or seems to be, arbitrary. This penchant for selfcriticism indicates the presence of some objective factor on which to base the decision to end a work. But such an objective factor is rarely to be found. This was a fact well known to Rouault. Recently, Michel Butor said that for him a work is finished when there is nothing more he can do for it except transmit it to others.[38]   Apparently, he can make such a decision without being bothered excessively by the belief that it is arbitrary and subjective, or perhaps he makes a decision in spite of such a belief.   For his part, Paul Valéry claimed that no artist worthy of the name could ever honestly say that a work is finished.[39]   The painter Georges Braque, on the other hand, told an interviewer that he always reached a point where the painting opposed its own resistance to the artist's manipulations.   In this case, it is not arbitrariness on the artist's part that makes him "call it a day," but rather the necessities of the situation once the artwork acquires a character of its own.   Braque claimed that at such a point it was impossible to go any further.[40]

As is obvious from the accounts of the critics Charensol, Courthion and Dorival, whether or not Rouault thought at length about what he was going to paint, his initial decision to start a painting was the result of a very strong emotional impulse.   As the first sketch was an outpouring of feeling, it is understandable that after putting it aside he would want to return to it again and again until he had realized its full potential. But by reworking it he might also spoil the intensity of the first state of the work; Claude Roger-Marx made an enlightening comment when he noted that Rouault's sketches and unfinished works were "completed in their incompletion" because the painter's sketches surpass works "that his dissatisfaction caused him to overdo."[41]

In L'Intemporel (1976), Malraux expressed some very novel and unorthodox views on the subject of sketches and their importance. According to him, it is a mistake to regard sketches as secondary, as mere drafts or preparations for other works. He argued that painters such as Rubens, Fragonard, Constable, Géricault, Delacroix, Corot, Daumier, Boudin and others, painted sketches which were not essentially preparatory studies, but which had another role to play. He believed that these sketches "suggest a search that their function does not justify" and added that "it would have been useless to press on with a preparatory study that had accomplished its purpose."[42]   For these reasons, Malraux believed that sketches were often another kind of painting, a pure painting so to speak, what he called "une peinture délivrée"—a liberated painting.   It was a kind of painting in which "the subject was in the service of painting itself and in which allusion replaced illusion" (p. 22).   He felt that the colors of these sketches had such an intensity that they did away with any idea of imitation, of notation, of reference to reality, and instead suggested what can only exist in the realm of the pictorial (p. 22).   He thought of such sketches as autonomous creations which tried to exhaust the transformative power of art and noted that in such cases, "the painter has traversed the mirror, reached the domain where forms and colors, invented by him rival those of reality, in order to become the notes of his own music" (p. 24).

It is interesting that some critics who had spoken of the "completeness of incompletion" in Rouault also spoke of the painter's unfinished works in a manner quite similar to the one Malraux would use in L'Intemporel, with his usual wealth of metaphors.   Rouault made use of figurative reality in his work in order to go beyond it to a spiritual one, and although his aim was not "pure painting," one can see that he too was part of the group of artists described by Malraux.   And although Malraux does not include Rouault in this group, his concept of "liberated painting" can apply to him as well as to Rubens, Fragonard et al.

Rouault himself was very conscious of the difficulties of his working method, and was quoted as having said: "I work and create like the passing wind or the blazing fire."   A critic has spoken of the "frenzy" and the "passion" of the artist and of his "violent reactions."   But this has to be supplemented by what Rouault wrote to Josef Florian.   He needed to work and rework his canvases over very long periods of time, to vary their forms and harmony until he could feel an inner satisfaction.[43]

It also appears that Rouault had to work and rework his paintings over a very long time because he was a fearful man as well as a bold one.[44]   He stated that he looked upon everything he produced with trepidation and confusion.   This would explain his impulse to work on canvases sporadically and then to put them aside for years, with the results that he left so many unfinished.   What Rouault needed to achieve was very obviously a sense of inner certitude about his works. This certitude did not come to him quickly or easily. He had to do a lot of groping, reflecting and waiting, and could never be certain that he would achieve what he desired. In this he resembled his revered teacher, the painter Gustave Moreau, who said to him that he believed in God alone and

> neither in what I touch or in what I see. I only believe in what I do not see and only in what I feel. My brain, my rationality seem to me ephemeral and of a doubtful reality. My inner feeling alone seems to me eternal and unquestionably certain. (Quoted in Georges Rouault, *Sur l'art et sur la vie*, p. 78).

****

The Russain-born painter Chaim Soutine (1893-1943) undoubtedly destroyed his works more systematically and on a larger scale than any other painter in history. He came to France sometime between 1911 and 1913 to study art and led a life of great poverty until December 1922, when the American collector Albert C. Barnes bought a large number of his paintings.

The art historians and critics Pierre Courthion and Monroe Wheeler have estimated that Soutine destroyed eight or nine out of every ten canvases he painted.[45] In 1929, the essayist and art historian Elie Faure wrote that the painter destroyed so much of his output because he was unable to paint as he wanted to. His ambition was to create works characterized by "equilibrium," harmony, balance and "exact proportions." Since he was unable to achieve this, he was divided against himself and saw no alternative but to destroy whatever failed to measure up to his ideal. The problem, of course, is to know what weight to accord Faure's hypothesis, which looks startling at first glance. Several critics have spoken of the painter's desire to be a classic, to follow in a tradition. Monroe Wheeler spoke of Soutine's "derivative" work, David Sylvester of "his paraphrases of the Old Masters" and Hilton Kramer of his "dreaming the dream of the museums."[46] Soutine's dissatisfaction with his work was in some measure due to his inability to equal those he admired.

One of the most convincing answers as to why Soutine destroyed so much of his work, especially that done in and prior to 1922-1923, was provided by a fellow painter, Jack Tworkov

(1900-1982).[47] He noted that the painter considered it necessary to capture "the sequence of ephemeral experience" during the time he was actually working on a canvas. If his changing response to the subject of the painting could not be set down to his satisfaction, in the time it took to make the painting, Soutine believed the canvas an unfaithful witness and a lie. He then proceeded to slash it into strips. He worked with the fear that emotion would fail him in the midst of a painting.

Monroe Wheeler was one of the first critics to note in his 1950 essay that around 1922 or 1923, Soutine developed a new style and acquired a mastery he had not previously enjoyed. With this newly acquired mastery came a facility which led to boredom, so that his desire to paint diminished. Wheeler felt that the artist "knew exactly what he intended, and changed his conception scarcely at all."[48]

In 1951, Clement Greenberg, who quoted Monroe Wheeler several times in his essay, proposed an additional solution to the problem posed by Soutine's case. According to Greenberg, Soutine finally realized that art, which is "ultimately social, its medium social-ness incarnate," could not lend itself to the expression of outright, total individualism which was this artist's project. To try to transcribe the expression of total individualism was an activity leading to the destruction of form. In order to avoid this,—it would be the destruction of his medium as well,—the painter had to compromise "by renouncing the fullness of his ambition and emotion."[49] The painter was caught between two incompatible situations, faced with choosing either the destruction of form or the renunciation of his most innate tendency, total self-expression. To Greenberg, it was a mistake to try to express emotions and feelings as the painter tried to do, because emotions, by their very nature, have an "extra-esthetic truth" and cannot be transcribed in their fullness, intensity or urgency. Were an artist successful in this transcription, he would destroy or overwhelm "form" and the medium which demands a discipline, a subordination to its rules. Greenberg did not actually say it, but he implied that Soutine had destroyed his paintings because he had "overwhelmed" form and his medium.

In a 1968 article on Soutine, Hilton Kramer also argued that the painter's "aspirations were impossible to realize."[50] He too saw Soutine as a man torn between contradictory tendencies: on the one hand towards classicism in the tradition of the masters and on the other towards an exacerbated Expressionism. Kramer noted that classicism is incompatible with the state of charged emotion characteristic of Soutine's work. He concluded that the artist asked too much of painting and agreed with Greenberg's statement to the effect that "Soutine set too high a value on the unimpeded expression of feeling." Paradoxically enough, Kramer thought it was precisely when the artist overvalued expression that his work was most unforgettable. But both critics felt it was a mistake to place so much emphasis on the expression of feeling since painting as a medium is not fit for it. Jack Tworkov, on the contrary, believed that painters can depict constantly changing feelings toward a model in what he called "the sequence of ephemeral experience." He noted the tremendous difficulties in transcribing this kind of experience but thought it could be done successfully, if only very rarely. He thought that Soutine's painting

> requires the unity of instantaneous perceiving and doing—a head-long rush which cannot be retarded for the elaboration of detail. It excludes touching up. If the artist fails, the failure is complete and disastrous. When he succeeds it is a miracle (p. 62).

As if anticipating the comments of later critics, Tworkov pointed out that the painter's preoccupation was not with the picture per se but rather with his attitudes and emotions toward his subject and with the depiction of the creative process itself. His highly incisive comments show that Soutine attempted precisely to destroy all of the paintings which were not "miracles"—all those he felt were either partial or complete failures.

Several critics have argued that what impelled Soutine to destroy his early work was his achievement of a greater technical facility and mastery around 1922-1923. He then attempted to do away with those earlier paintings which did not measure up to his later achievement, and which only had an "experimental" and cathartic value.[51] All of the people who knew Soutine well speak of the fact that he tracked down his early work with a vengeance, buying it back whenever he could, exchanging later paintings for earlier ones in order to destroy them.[52] He did not wait many years to develop a hatred of his early work, particularly those pictures done in Céret around 1919-1922; Peter Stone, who visited the town in 1969, was told by one of its inhabitants that she remembered seeing the painter and his dealer, Zborowski, "make a bonfire of the pictures."[53] Monroe Wheeler related that when Zborowski visited Céret, he saw the painter attempting to set fire to his paintings. According to all witnesses, Soutine's destruction of his work was habitual and by no means confined to work produced in any one place or at any one time, although he did have a special hatred of everything he had done at Céret.

Another factor should be noted in explaining Soutine's habit of destroying so much of his work. The people who knew him all commented on his self-doubt, his difficulty in accepting criticism, his lack of faith in his own judgment. All agree that, without the approval of someone he trusted, he more often than not, would destroy what he had done. He also refused to have an exhibit in his lifetime. We do not know whether this self-doubt was due to his inability to paint in the classical manner, or to a sense that he was not master of his art, or to his inability to go beyond a certain level of achievement.

Monroe Wheeler suggested that with the advent of "mastery" came a falling off both in the intensity and quantity of Soutine's production. According to the critics, mastery of his art caused the painter as many problems as his lack of it had done prior to 1922-1923. This irony is surpassed by two others—that a painter whose works show such strength and force should have had so many doubts about his work, and that so many people continue to prefer the Céret paintings to most others in Soutine's *oeuvre*.

Perhaps it is not so much a question of control. After the explosive, uninhibited paintings done at Céret, Soutine could not continue in the same vein. He had exhausted his emotional energy, and had come to the end of a particular phase of his development. He himself admitted to being depressed and demoralized in a 1923 letter to Zborowski. At the time he was in Cagnes, just after leaving Céret. He hated Cagnes, couldn't do any work, and couldn't seem to find any subjects he could respond to. He even asked Zborowski to advise him as to where he should go next to find subjects for his work.[54]

Soutine continued to destroy his work on a large scale even after he acquired the mastery the critics speak of. If he destroyed eight or nine of every ten paintings, obviously he went on with his purges even after having gotten rid of a large number of the Céret canvases. In retrospect, of course, it can be seen that even if Soutine did acquire great mastery of his art around 1923, this was not evident to him. If there was a falling-off in his production, it was undoubtedly a cause of anguish to him, as he probably believed that after the outpouring of 1922-1923, the source had begun to run dry.

Some critics feel that the Céret paintings were done before Soutine acquired the mastery they speak of. But these canvases are not the work of an artist who is not fully master of his art. Soutine's hatred of these canvases may be due not only to the fact that he considered them technically inferior, but that they represented a mode of painting he had left behind. It may be that he pursued his attempts to destroy them because he felt they were too personal in character and not squarely in the classical tradition which he wanted to follow. Elie Faure's remarks concerning Soutine's desire to be a "classical" artist must be taken seriously, as Faure himself knew the painter. Certainly the destruction of Soutine's best work is only one example, neither the first nor the last (as the case of Giacometti and De Kooning show), of an artist destroying some of his best work for reasons he alone considered valid.

****

It is difficult to estimate the number of sculptures and paintings destroyed by Alberto Giacometti (1901-1966), but from the remarks made by his friends and acquaintances it is likely to have been very high. Yet Thomas B. Hess, who interviewed him many times, wrote: " . . . he accomplished enough to fill three careers."[55]

Giacometti destroyed so much of his work for many reasons, but it is hard to accord primary importance to any one of these or to determine the order in which they should be considered. The emphasis placed on the importance of each could vary with one's interpretation.

Giacometti began his career (as he himself said) by trying to copy or represent what he saw, but soon realized that this was easier said than done. As he observed in an interview, "On ne voit la réalité qu'à travers des écrans" (One sees reality only through screens).[56] In this interview he observed that although everyone thinks he knows what a head is, people do not in fact have such knowledge: when they look at a head they see only a "greco-roman bust." What we see is only a mediated vision, coming to us through screens, that is through another's art or through preconceptions and prejudgments. Giacometti felt very strongly the need to dispell the influence of the vision imposed on us by habit or familiarity; he considered it imperative to acquire a pristine, personal vision. This reminds us of Cézanne's statement that artists had to forget all previous works of art.[57]

But reaching such a vision is an extremely difficult enterprise, and in his attempt to do so, Giacometti undoubtedly destroyed many of his works. He told André Parinaud that, in his youth at least, the longer he looked at the model, the thicker became the screen between the model's reality and himself. He added that he began by seeing the model, but little by little sculptures interposed themselves between model and sculptor. His vision of the model then disappeared and the model's head became that of an unknown person; he was no longer sure either of its appearance, of its dimensions, or of anything at all. The statement that there were too many sculptures between the model and himself could mean that too many memories of already existing works hampered his attempts to sculpt in an original manner. It could also mean that he had in mind too many possible ways of executing the sculpture and was unable to choose among them. When he finally succeeded in seeing the reality before him, he was hard put to render it because if he looked at the model full face he forgot the profile, whereas if he looked at the profile he forgot the face. He added that everything became discontinuous and he could not seize the whole. There were too many levels of reality, which became too complex and ungraspable. One of the reasons for this was that his vision changed every day. He saw either a face in its weighty geometry, or the face as a blot, or as a detail, or the whole face. This led him, for a time, to abandon the idea of sculpting or painting what he saw, and he gave up the practice of working with a model. From about 1925 to 1935 he worked from memory.[58]

For Giacometti, the failure to reproduce reality was not only his personal failure as an artist but something even more serious. In the 1962 interview with André Parinaud he noted that he sculpted in an effort to understand what he saw. He had already made the same statement to Peter Selz.[59] Seeing for him was not a passive act. When he looked too hard and long, the object or person began to disappear and he ended up not knowing what he was looking at. Each time he approached reality, he felt it pulling away from him; he could not get close enough to it to examine and understand it. For Giacometti, to *know* what he saw, to *understand* it and *feel* it, it was necessary to paint or sculpt. He told an interviewer that "resemblance is what makes me discover the exterior world."[60]   He felt that by discovering the exterior world he could get out of the prison constituted by the inner one. But the problem with the exterior world was that, as he said to another interviewer: "Si je veux copier comme je vois, ça disparaît." (If I want to copy the way I see, it disappears).[61]   He also believed that reality projects itself in a partial and unstable manner; grasping it was for him an impossibility. He said to an interviewer that what modern artists sought was to grasp something which constantly eluded them.   What they wanted to possess was not reality itself but the impression or feelings they had of reality.[62]

But even the very sensation of reality kept disappearing in his effort to grasp, understand and represent it. That reality projects itself in an unstable, doubtful or partial manner he explained by saying that when he looked at a glass on a table, he copied the "residue of a vision" but not the reality of the object itself (Parinaud, p. 9). Each time he looked at the glass he was copying, there came to him a glimpse of its color, shape or light, something very hard to fix, which could be approximated only by a little line or spot. When he looked at the glass again, after having put down the line or spot, he had the feeling that the glass was in the process of recomposing itself as if it had lost its reality when he looked away. It appeared to him that the line or spot he put down each time he took his eyes off the model caused a break in his contact with the model or reality. The reality of the glass thus became doubtful because its projection in his mind was partial. He could not paint the glass in its wholeness; only through hundreds of approximate lines or spots could he ever hope to constitute its appearance (Parinaud, p. 9).

Similarly, he had great difficulty in determining how far he should stand from his model. He felt this problem acutely when he went back to working with a model around 1935, after about ten years of doing without one. He said to an interviewer (December 1955) that very early he had realized that his work had no connection at all with the model he saw. To facilitate matters, he placed the model further away, but when he did so the sculpture became smaller and smaller. This phenomenon was related to his sense that reality pulled further away from him the closer he tried to come to it. Because of this, reality seemed unstable and impossible to grasp. He was intent on achieving what he called "the illusion of reality, of appearance—of absolute appearance." As he told David Sylvester, an artist cannot merely reproduce what he sees, he must also reproduce the whole atmosphere, the ambiance of what he has seen and felt.[63]

In an interview with Pierre Dumayet in 1963, Giacometti spoke of his portrait of Professor Isaku Yanaihara. He said that after working on it all day long, he used to feel in the evening that it was good work (this happened every day for several months). But the more he went on with the painting, the more the subject disappeared. (Giacometti had made the same statement, concerning another model, in his 1962 interview). The day of the Professor's departure, he remembered having said to him: "If I draw one more line, the canvas will abolish itself completely." He was chagrined to see that what he wanted to copy disappeared before his eyes. Giacometti once said that by dint of looking at the model, he no longer saw it. This prompted the interviewer to ask: "If you don't recognize your brother or your wife, how can your portraits of them resemble them?" (Dumayet, p. 43). He also stated in this interview that making a painting or sculpture of what he saw no longer entered his mind. What he worked for was to understand why he couldn't succeed in making a work that resembled the model.[64]

In a conversation in 1963, Giacometti explained that he had begun his career by trying to do a whole figure with legs, a head, and arms, but everything seemed to him wrong and false; he didn't believe in what he had done. In order to make his work more precise, he was forced to make sacrifices, to reduce it. Thus he eliminated the legs and the arms. At the end there remained only a plaque on which there were just two hollows: the vertical and horizontal found in all figures. Looking at the result of all his labor, he used to be quite disappointed to think that his mastery came down to so little. He also told the interviewer, (something he had already said to others), that he would work only in order to find out why he failed. Finishing a statue or painting didn't even enter his mind, and whether he succeeded or not was the least of his concerns.[65]

To other interviewers—Georges Charbonnier (1965), André Parinaud (1962) and Mercedes Matter (1965)—he said that the work itself was of little importance, that what really mattered was what he himself felt, learned and experienced while sculpting or painting. The question of the destruction of his work came up specifically in the interview with André Parinaud (June 1962). He explained to this interviewer that when he started to work he had not one second's hesitation in undoing the work of the day before, because every day he saw further. If after a working session he saw things better, more clearly or saw reality even slightly differently, then even if the painting or sculpture didn't make much sense or was destroyed—he felt he had won. He gained a new sensation, one he had never experienced before. This sensation was therefore without any equivalent and was more important to him than the product. He added that he was indifferent to posterity and to leaving behind any works of art. Speaking of the destruction of his work, he said that it was not really complete destruction because in everything he does an artist gains knowledge, skill and understanding for use later.

Giacometti's destructive impulses have been viewed in a somewhat different light by the poet Jacques Dupin, among others. Dupin believed that the sculptor's need to destroy "conditioned his creative activity."[66] Dupin gave two reasons for his assertion. First, he felt that recourse to violence and destruction was a means, "to provoke an encounter with the impossible" (p. 18). Giacometti's relationship with reality and with art "are fraught with violence in proportion to the dissatisfaction to which they reduce him" (p. 18). Second, Dupin believed that the multiplication of lines on a canvas was a way of refusing to give significance and certainty to any one line. He added that we find "la contestation," the constant putting of everything into question, as the very principle of creativity in this artist. It is true that Giacometti, by the multiplication of lines, managed to have each line contradict the effect of the previous one. He thus opened a "contradictory debate among them." Additional lines never settled it but only continued it (p. 32).

When one reads the article written by Professor Isaku Yanaihara and the book by James Lord, both of whom sat for portraits by Giacometti, the accuracy of Dupin's explanation becomes quite evident. This is a typical example of what the painter repeatedly told both his sitters:

> Only another little effort, I feel very near the truth. Five minutes ago your face was almost finished. It was a portrait so beautiful that I felt like showing it to you. Even the eyes were perfect. But now it isn't there any more. There is nothing left on the canvas.[67]

James Lord had exactly the same experience as Professor Yanaihara when he later sat for a portrait by Giacometti. He made it clear in his book that the painter tried to capture "a reality that was as identical as possible to the vision he had of it."[68] The painter tried to give a representation of his vision of reality but at the same time insisted that he believed it essential to work without any preconception, "without knowing in advance what the picture is going to look like" (Lord, p. 45). This statement and many like it prove that the words "vision" and "conception," as Giacometti used them, should not be taken in any but the most general sense.

From the account given by James Lord, it is clear that the painter destroyed his works almost as systematically as did Soutine, and essentially for the same reasons. Like him Giacometti insisted that he had to approximate or render the feelings he experienced while working on a canvas or sculpture. Each day when he went to work, he was unable to go on with what he had accomplished earlier, as the reality of his "vision," or his feelings, had changed. Every single day that he worked on a painting or sculpture was a new challenge. This is why James Lord writes: " . . . he is obliged to feel that it is necessary to start his entire career over again every day, as it were, from scratch" (p. 28). Every time Giacometti worked, it was as if he were doing so for the first time. He could not help transforming and obliterating the image that was already on the canvas. Because his view of things changed, his works had to change too. This is exactly why Soutine insisted on finishing a canvas in one sitting, as he also knew that if he returned to it later, he would not see it in the same way.

Both painters refused to be imprisoned by a view which could only be that of a particular time and place. Their view changed too often and too fast for them to commit themselves to it. James Lord summarizes this by saying of Giacometti: "This is one of the reasons why he so often feels that the particular sculpture or painting on which he happens to be working at the moment is that one which will for the very first time express what he subjectively experiences in response to an objective reality" (p. 18).

Dupin's ideas concerning "la contestation," and the painter's constant transformation and obliteration of the images on his canvases, should be seen in the context of a remark made by Giacometti in an interview with the late Thomas Hess. He was troubled, he said, by the fact that a work always contained more than one "sensation." In sculpture, for instance, there was what he called "the image I can see"—obviously the model he worked with. But he was also conscious of another image, one he couldn't see, the "vision" or "conception" he felt. He called this "the image I can't see, the one I must struggle to find and am always losing. Both in the same sculpture."[69] From reading the accounts of Professor Yanaihara and James Lord, it becomes obvious that the painter would have experienced less anxiety had he been able to finish a canvas in a single sitting, or at most a few. Both write that on several occasions they saw a finished work on the canvas, only to have Giacometti sit down to change and finally obliterate it.

Giacometti could probably not be satisfied with a work painted in one sitting or in a few, because he had an aversion to anything that came too easily. He said that when things went well he did not feel challenged, but bored. Therefore, he may not only have destroyed those works he considered bad but also some very good ones, simply because he distrusted the ease with which he had done them.

Like Rouault, Giacometti had a problem knowing when to stop. The portraits of Isaku Yanaihara and James Lord were never actually "finished;" the sitters finally had to leave Paris and could no longer spare the time to pose for the painter. The problem of when to stop was complicated by the fact that Giacometti believed a painting was never finished. He said this in so many words to Alexander Watt.[70] He made the statement because he felt that certainty about a work was unattainable. This was due in large part to the difficulty of grasping as a coherent whole what David Sylvester excellently summarizes as

> the accumulation of memories none of which is quite the same as any other, because each of them is affected by what has gone before, by the continually changing relation between all that has already been put down and the next glance at the model.[71]

In fact, he told James Lord that Cézanne too didn't finish many works, but rather abandoned and destroyed them. This, he said, was because the master didn't want to be limited by any one point of view, or continue working on a painting after his feeling about it had changed. One has the impression from what Giacometti said about Cézanne's abandoning his works that the latter could not sort out his "accumulation of memories" or integrate new ones into a painting—whether or not he had worked on it for a long period of time. What Giacometti didn't say was that for Cézanne it was nature that changed continually, and too quickly for the artist to have a fair chance of setting down what he saw or remembered of it.

Giacometti's experience shows that originality can sometimes be more of a liability than an asset. He was certainly one of the most original artists of the twentieth century. His way of seeing and approaching reality was special because he did not have a matter-of-fact assurance toward it.   In defamiliarizing it he transformed it to such a degree that he felt lost, unable to formulate another way of seeing things and making them hang together. He was in a no man's land where traditional points of view no longer worked; he had to grope to find new ones. This was because the reality he painted became uncertain: "its projection in my head is uncertain or partial."

Giacometti claimed that he did not paint his vision of things but a residue of this vision as well as his consciousness of it. This consciousness was uncertain and fragmented. The disconcerting, puzzling aspect of what one sees is one of the elements the Cubist painters had sought to paint. What appeared to them a valid method of composition—representation of divergent perceptions and points of view—seemed undesirable to Giacometti. He wanted to give a whole, fully integrated representation but could not succeed—he found his vision too volatile. As a result, he neither had nor could have a theory to help him fit the discontinuous nature of what he saw into a unified pattern. Each brushstroke was disconnected from the previous one due to the fragmentary nature of his perceptions and to their differences.

Giacometti believed that artists want to possess their experience of reality rather than reality itself. But this sensation is too elusive and cannot be grasped. While the Impressionists, the Fauves and the Cubists believed that it was possible to render the equivalent of one's impressions, Giacometti did not. The connection between reality and one's impression of it was too tenuous. This made it impossible for him to believe in the likelihood of giving reality a form.

The most succint statement about Giacometti, and one which best captures his frustration, comes from Michel Leiris:

Never closed off, a drawing by Giacometti offers the image of almost his entire art; a quest to approach some very simple realities, which even if one could snare them, it would be out of the question to set down once and for all, because—in the account an artist can give of them—they must bear the mark of a hesitation, of an incompletion or be abstractions and realities, at once near and strange, from which we cannot separate the incertitude of the relationship we have with them.[72]

****

In a letter dated 1885 to his fiancee Martha Bernays, Freud, then 29, wrote that he had destroyed all his notes, papers, manuscripts and letters (except those written by her). He explained that he had done this for several reasons. One was that since his "thoughts and feelings" about the world and himself had changed completely, the materials he destroyed were no longer pertinent. He indicated that the destruction of his papers would lead him to re-examine and restructure his ideas and that he would start again from scratch. He stated that everything "that lies beyond the great turning point of my life, beyond our love and my choice of profession, died long ago and must not be deprived of a worthy funeral." With his marriage he was embarking on a new life; since the past was now dead he felt justified in destroying all the papers belonging to it.

He also remarked in this letter that the amount of material was so huge that, had he not burned it, he would almost have been buried under its mass as "that stuff settles round me like sand drifts round the Sphinx . . . " He offered another reason for his actions: "I couldn't have matured or died without worrying about who would get hold of those old papers."[73]

Evidently Freud already felt in 1895, before he had written any of his major works, that any potentially damaging evidence had to be destroyed lest it one day be used against him. His remarks lead to a great many speculations and suspicions about the content of what he destroyed. Why did he himself not realize the suspicions such an act might give rise to? We do not know. Certainly, he could not have imagined, in 1885, the place that his work would eventually assume in the history of ideas. But he did not stop destroying his letters, notebooks, manuscripts and notes; he repeated his act in 1907. At that time he

moved to a new apartment and, according to his biographer, Ernest Jones, he did not really have room to keep all of the accumulated material.[74]   By then Freud was, of course, much better
known than in 1885 and everything he destroyed was of far
greater importance in the corpus of his work.

These repeated acts of destruction of personal papers suggest that Freud may have considered that particularly damaging
material might later be used against him in particular and
against the theories of psychoanalysis in general.   Better to prevent any such situation by obliterating the material, which, in-
criminating or not, might cause problems.   He may also have
feared that prolonged arguments would waste his time and
energy.   He was, as his biographers Sachs, Fromm, Brome and
Mannoni make clear, authoritarian and intolerant to the point
that he did not want to reply to arguments from others.

Recently, Frank J. Sulloway has addressed himself to the
question of Freud's destruction of material of great importance
for the history of psychoanalysis, and for the history of ideas in
general:

> Hence Freud actively sought to cultivate the unknown about him-
> self to ensure that he, as intellectual hero, would not be devalued
> by an overly detailed understanding of his genius. Even in his own
> lifetime this strategy had its benefits. To remain inscrutable, even
> if only in part, was to preserve an atmosphere of mystery about him-
> self that in turn prompted awe and respect among those who joined
> his movement.[75]

Freud himself states in his *Autobiographical Study* (1924)
that the public has no further "claim" on his personal life.   He
adds that he has been more open and frank in his writings than
others—a cause for regret.[76]   He is defending himself here
against any accusation of withholding from the public material
essential to an understanding of his theories.   He is also asserting
that he himself is the sole judge of what the public should know
about him.

According to Jung, who had reproached Freud for not giving him enough material to conduct an analysis of him, and
insisted that the founder of psychoanalysis give him more details on his thoughts and his private life, Freud answered: "No, I
can't risk my authority."[77]   Clearly, Sulloway is right in stating
that Freud did not want to dispel the "inscrutability" he maintained.

Not all scholars believe the statement made by Jung and charge the latter with ill-will and bias.[78]   Philip Rieff, for example, speaks of Freud's willingness to pronounce judgments and draw out the evidence for them from his own life as well as from clinical data."[79]   There was therefore a problem of how much information concerning the private life to make available: in other words, where to draw the line.

Statements like Rieff's make one wonder if Freud's method of working did not finally impel him to destroy material he considered too personal. There is no doubt, in view of the statement he makes in his 1924 *Autobiographical Study*, that he was afraid critics would read his notebooks and interpret their content as reflecting their author's psychological problems.   They might then claim that his theories were designed to justify himself in his own eyes. This would only place in doubt the broader applicability of his theories.

It is probably largely due to this fear that Freud did not want the letters to his one time confident Wilhelm Fliess, which contained so much material regarding his self-analysis, to fall into the wrong hands. This led him to try to get back those letters after Fliess' death. One can understand Mrs. Fliess' fears that Freud might recover them, as she was sure he would burn them. For the same reasons, Princess Marie Bonaparte refused to turn the letters to Fliess over to Freud, who had requested that she do so. If he went to such lengths to recover materials like the letters to Fliess, it is undoubtedly because he feared that theories based on materials drawn from his own life would be labeled unscientific. One scholar, Marthe Robert, has already said more or less the same thing.[80]

If psychoanalysis is the scientific endeavor that Freud claimed it was, it is hard to understand why he did not leave his notes and manuscripts intact, so that others might understand his thoughts and the *données* of the problems he addressed. Few scientists burn their notes and any such action can only raise suspicions about a scientist's motives.

Freud's clinical data and the use to which he put them also present some problems. In his monumental work, Henri Ellenberger writes:

> Depth psychology can be understood as the combined findings from Freud's self-analysis and the analysis of his patients. In his mind the findings confirmed each other and confirmed much of the theory of neurosis and the model of the mind he had previously formulated.[81]

If Ellenberger is correct, Freud "formulated the theory of neurosis and the model of the mind" before he had done much clinical work. He did not work out the theories from a large body of data based on direct experience with patients, and this is one fact he obviously might not have wanted to be generally known. Paul Roazen states that "Ferenczi once maintained that he [Freud] had at his disposal 'the minimal numbers of cases necessary for a generalization, namely two.' "[82] He goes on to quote Freud:

> Naturally a single case does not give us all the information that we should like to have, or, to put it more correctly, it might teach us everything, if we were only in a position to make everything out.[83]

Roazen also discusses the criticism of those who charge Freud with reductionism and oversimplification on the one hand, and with incomplete and unsystematic research on the other. He notes in this regard:

> Much of the criticism of Freud's case histories has failed to remember this issue of reductionism; each case was written not with the intention of exhausting the clinical realities, but in order to establish particular theoretical principles (p. 87).

He also quotes several statements by Freud which make it clear that he, Freud, did not pretend to be systematic and comprehensive in his research (p. 87). But an explanation of such a working method should point out that analysts, in many cases, believed patients to be cured only to find that the patients had relapsed months or years later. Freud and others might not have made such judgments if they had more evidence drawn from clinical data; material showing this could well have been included in the destroyed notes.

Freud's account of patients' revelations may not be accurate or free of ideological bias or prejudice caused by theoretical beliefs. It is quite true that he admitted to one error concerning the so-called seduction theory, because he was led to believe statements made by patients. It is also possible that he was deceived more than once by such clinical material, at least until he had enough experience with patients to recognize patterns in the information they provided.

Freud considered himself a scientist; he hoped that what he had written would stand on its own coherence, logic and truth, without reference to himself. But Roazen quotes a very interesting passage from a letter that Freud wrote to Fliess: "A man like me cannot live without a hobby-horse, a consuming passion—in Schiller's words a tyrant. I have found my tyrant and in his service I know no limits. My tyrant is psychology."[84]

Another statement, to the effect that his life was of interest only because of its relationship to psychoanalysis, has a very ambiguous ring.[85] It could mean that his refusal to give details about his private life and his inner thoughts was justified because only his work mattered. (Besides, he had given the public all the information he felt was needed in the works he mentioned in the 1924 *Autobiographical Study*, namely *The Interpretation of Dreams* and *The Psychology of Everyday Life*). But if one takes into account his statement to Fliess about his tyrant being psychology, then it turns out that his work and his life are much more closely interconnected than one would infer from what he wrote in 1924 when he claimed he was much more open and frank than others. Freud could not decide, it appears, whether his work had a scientific, objective value independent of the personality of the man who had written the books. At least one critic believes that "Freud himself soon ceased to anchor his increasingly fanciful speculations even to anecdotal evidence from clinical observation."[86] Such a viewpoint, of course, means an absolute rejection of the scientific value of Freud's work, and implies that its chief interest lies in its connection with the man who created it. Another critic speaks of the "vast array of refutation-avoiding devices which permeate Freud's writings."[87] This statement too, if taken to its logical end, means that the private individual interfered too much in the exposition of impersonal, scientific theories and that, regrettably, criticism of Freud's work must involve criticism of the man.

The Swiss psychiatrist Eugen Bleuler (1857-1939) could not understand why his more famous contemporary thought it so important that his whole "edifice" should be "accepted." In a letter to Freud he pointed out that any scientific theory is challenged, discussed, contradicted, corrected and changed. It wasn't clear to him why Freud had such difficulty accepting this fact. Bleuler went on to say however, that Freud's contribution was certainly a fundamental one. He added that he remembered once having told him: "Psychologically you impress me as an artist."[88]

The only explanation that Bleuler could give for Freud's

apparent inability to stand the idea of scrutiny and perhaps skepticism on the part of the scientific community, was Freud's artistic temperament. He was a creator who couldn't bear to have his "art product" dissected by critics. It is doubtful that Bleuler knew of his colleague's destruction of his letters and notes, but his explanation is certainly a very cogent one. One of the axioms of esthetics has always been that art should conceal art; Freud would certainly not be the first creative individual to have burned his notes with the idea of eradicating all traces of the trials and tribulations he underwent in bringing forth his work. He thought that the scope and import of his ideas would be diminished or weakened by discussion of their origin in and relationship to his private life. Like Flaubert, Wordsworth, Kafka and others, he did not want to show the extent to which his attitudes, views and prejudices were present in his work. Like many of the artists whose problems we have discussed, he was quite concerned with being in firm control of his work and wished to present it in such a manner that nothing would detract from the impact it made.

Notes

1 *Lettres à Madame Hanska*, I, 309.

2 *Letters to Felice*, ed. Erich Heller and Jürgen Born, trans. James Stern and Elizabeth Duckworth (New York: Schocken Books, 1973), p. 314.

3 See *I Am a Memory Come Alive*, ed. Nahum Glatzer (New York: Schocken Books, 1974), p. xiii.

4 *I Am a Memory Come Alive*, p. 239.

5 Maurice Blanchot, "Kafka et Brod," *Nouvelle Revue Française*, no. 22, octobre 1954, p. 697.

6 Nahum Glatzer, *I Am a Memory Come Alive*, p. xi.

7 Gustav Janouch, *Conversations with Franz Kafka* (New York: New Directions, 1971), p. 150.

8 Franz Kafka, *Letters to Friends, Family and Editors*, trans. Richard and Clara Winston (New York: Schocken Books, 1977), p. 387.

9 *Letters to Felice*, October 1, 1917, p. 545.

10 *Letters to Felice*, pp. 20-21, 138, 245, 304, 307-308, 313, 420, 437-438.

11 Letter of July 5, 1923 in *Letters to Friends, Family and Editors*, pp.

332-335. Another translation of the same letter appears in *I Am a Memory Come Alive*, pp. 223-225.

[12] See *Dearest Father: Stories and Other Writings*, trans. Ernst Kaiser and Eithne Wilkins (New York: Schocken Books, 1954), p. 270.

[13] *I Am a Memory Come Alive*, p. 198.

[14] *I Am a Memory Come Alive*, p. 238.

[15] *The New Grove Dictionary of Music and Musicians*, ed. Stanley Sadie (New York: MacMillian, 1980), Vol. II, 690-693.

[16] G. W. Hopkins, *The New Grove Dictionary of Music and Musicians*, II, 692.

[17] *Correspondance de Paul Dukas*, ed. Georges Favre (Paris: Editions Durand et Cie., 1971), p. 157.

[18] The information that the destroyed works were entirely or almost entirely finished was given by Frédéric de la Grandville and Marc Vignal in their article on Dukas in *Larousse de la Musique* (Paris: Larousse, 1982), p. 490 and by Dukas' friend Gustave Samazeuilh, *La Revue Musicale*, mai-juin 1936, p. 21.

[19] Georges Favre, *L'Oeuvre de Paul Dukas* (Paris: Durand et Cie., 1969), p. 21.

[20] *La Revue Musicale*, mai-juin 1936, p. 25.

[21] Letter to Robert Brussel, *La Revue Musicale*, mai-juin 1936, p. 28. This letter is dated February 19, 1915.

[22] *The New York Times*, obituary article on Rouault, February 14, 1958.

[23] See "L'Affaire Rouault," *Gazette des Beaux-Arts*, avril 1974, Supplément, p. 2. Waldemar George et Geneviève Nouaille-Rouault, *L'Univers de Rouault* (Paris: Scrépel, 1971), p. 77.

[24] Pierre Courthion, *Georges Rouault* (New York: Harry N. Abrams, 1962), p. 295.

[25] Georges Chabot, *Hommage to Georges Rouault* (New York: Tudor Publishing Co., 1971), p. 56. Maurice Coutot, *Gazette des Beaux-Arts*, avril 1974, Supplement, p. 2.

[26] Pierre Descargues, *Arts, Lettres, Spectacles*, 21 mars 1947, p. 1, 3.

[27] François Chapon, *Oeuvre Gravé de Rouault*. Texte de François Chapon. 2 vols. Catalogue établi par Isabelle Rouault avec la collaboration d'Olivier Nouaille-Rouault (Monte Carlo: Editions André Sautet, 1978), p. 18.

[28] Jacques Lassaigne, *Dictionnaire de la peinture moderne* (Paris: Hazan, 1954), p. 252.

[29] Waldemar George et Geneviève Nouaille-Rouault, *L'Univers de Rouault*, p. 88.

[30] Pierre Courthion, p. 295.

[31] Pierre Courthion, p. 296.

[32] *Correspondance Georges Rouault-André Suarès* (Paris: Gallimard, 1960), 81-82.

[33] Bernard Dorival, "Préface," Georges Rouault. *Oeuvres inachevées données à l'Etat*. (Paris: Consorts Rouault, 1964), p. 14.

[34] Pierre Courthion, "Rouault au Louvre," *Arts, Lettres, Spectacles*, 24 au 30 juin 1964, p. 9.

[35] Georges Charensol, "Rouault: peintures inconnues ou célèbres," *Revue des deux mondes*," 1er avril 1965, p. 452. Claude Roger-Marx, "Rouault au Louvre," *Revue de Paris*, août-septembre 1964, p. 145.

36 Lassaigne, *Dictionnaire de la peinture moderne*, p. 253; Courthion, *Rouault*, p. 255.

37 Courthion, *Rouault*, p. 300; Claude Roger-Marx, p. 144.

38 See "Les Modifications de Michel Butor: entretien avec Antoine de Gaudemar," *Magazine Littéraire*, no. 191, Janvier 1981, p. 84.

39 Valéry, *Oeuvres* II, 1232-1233.

40 André Verdet, *Entretiens, notes et écrits sur la peinture* (Paris: Editions Galilée, 1978), p. 45.

41 "Rouault au Louvre," *Revue de Paris*, août-septembre 1964, p. 145.

42 André Malraux, *L'Intemporel* (Paris: Gallimard, 1976), p. 22.

43 G. Marchiori, *Rouault* (New York: Reynal & Co., William Morrow & Co., n.d.), p. 17. Rouault's unpublished letter to Josef Florian is quoted by François Chapon, *Oeuvre Gravé de Rouault*, p. 20.

44 *Correspondance Georges Rouault-André Suarès*, p. 229.

45 Pierre Courthion, *Soutine, peintre du déchirant* (Lausanne: Edita-Denoël, 1972), p. 62. Monroe Wheeler, *Soutine* (New York: Museum of Modern Art, 1950), p. 88.

46 Monroe Wheeler, p. 79. *David Sylvester*, p. 4. Hilton Kramer, p. 230.

47 "The Wandering Soutine," *Art News*, November 1950, pp. 30-33, 62.

48 Monroe Wheeler, p. 79.

49 Clement Greenberg, "Chaim Soutine," *Partisan Review*, no. 1 (January-February 1951), p. 87.

50 Hilton Kramer, "Soutine and the Problem of Expressionism," *The Age of the Avant-Garde* (New York: Farrar, Strauss and Giroux, 1973), p. 229.

51 David Sylvester, *Soutine* (Arts Council of Great Britain, 1963), pp. 5-6. This essay was reprinted in *C. Soutine* (Arts Council of Great Britain, 1981). Monroe Wheeler, *Soutine*, 1950. Raymond Cogniat, *Soutine* (Paris: Flammarion, 1973), p. 17.

52 Marcelin Castaing and Jean Leymarie, *Soutine*, trans. John Ross (New York: Harry N. Abrams, 1962), p. 12. Gerda Michaelis Groth (Mademoiselle Garde), *Mes Années avec Soutine* (Paris: Denoël, 1973), p. 126. Andrée Collié, "Souvenirs sur Soutine," *Le Spectateur des Arts*, décembre 1944, pp. 17-18.

53 Peter Stone, "Soutine at Céret," *Art and Artists*, April 1970, p. 56.

54 Soutine's letter was quoted by Raymond Cogniat, *Soutine* , trans. Eileen B. Hennessy (New York: Crown Publishers, 1973), p. 66.

55 "Alberto Giacometti," *Art News*, March 1966, p. 35.

56 Interview with Alain Jouffroy, *Arts, Lettres, Spectacles*, no. 545, decembre 1955, p. 9.

57 Quoted in Bernard Dorival, *Cézanne* (Paris: Tisne, 1948), pp. 2, 6.

58 André Parinaud, "Entretien avec Alberto Giacometti," *Arts, Lettres, Spectacles*, no. 873, 13-19 juin, 1962, pp. 1,5.

59 Peter Selz, *New Images of Man*, (New York: Museum of Modern Art, 1959).

60 Georges Charbonnier, "Alberto Giacometti," *Le Monologue du peintre*, vol. I (Paris: Julliard, 1959), p. 172.

61 Pierre Dumayet, *Vu et entendu*, (Paris: Stock, 1964), p. 43.

62 André Parinaud, *Arts, Lettres, Spectacles*, no. 871, p. 9.

63 Interview with David Sylvester, *L'Ephémère*, no. 18, automne 1971, Galerie Maeght.

64 Pierre Dumayet, p. 43.

65 Jean Clay, *Visages de l'art moderne* (Lausanne: Edtions Rencontre, 1969), p.

66 Jacques Dupin, *Alberto Giacometti*, (Maeght, 1962), p. 17.

67 Isaku Yanaihara, "Pages de journal," *Derrière le miroir* (Maeght, 1961, p. 23.

68 James Lord, "Alberto Giacometti," *L'Oeil*, no. 1 (janvier 1955), p. 19, and *A Giacometti Portrait* (New York: Museum of Modern Art, 1965), pp. 6, 15, 23, 28, 29, 62.

69 Thomas Hess, "Alberto Giacometti," *Art News*, May 1958, p. 67.

70 "Conversation with Giacometti," *Arts*, no. 4 (1960), pp. 100-102.

71 David Sylvester, "The Residue of a Vision," *Alberto Giacometti*, Arts Council of Great Britain, Tate Gallery Exhibit, London, 1965, p. 27.

72 Michel Leiris, *Alberto Giacometti, dessins* (Paris: Galerie Claude Bernard, 1975), p. 14.

73 *The Letters of Sigmund Freud*, trans. Tania and James Stern, ed. Ernst L. Freud (New York: Basic Books, 1960), p. 140.

74 Ernest Jones, *The Life and Work of Sigmund Freud*, vol. I (New York: Basic Books, 1981), p. xii.

75 Frank Sulloway, *Freud: Biologist of the Mind* (New York: Basic Books, 1979), pp. 7-8.

76 *Works of Sigmund Freud*, Standard Edition, vol. XX, p. 73.

77 Carl Jung, *Memories, Dreams, Reflections*, trans. A. and C. Winston (New York: Pantheon Books, 1961, 1963), p. 158.

78 Giovanni Costigan, *Freud: A Short Biography* (New York: MacMillan, 1965), p. 162.

79 Philip Rieff, Freud: *The Mind of the Moralist* (New York: Viking Press, 1959), p. 27.

80 Marthe Robert, *From Oedipus to Moses*, trans. Ralph Manheim (New York: Anchor Books, 1976), pp. 97-98.

81 Henri Ellenberger, *The Discovery of the Unconscious: The History and Evolution of Dynamic Psychiatry* (New York: Basic Books, 1970), p. 490.

82 Paul Roazen, *Freud: Political and Social Thought* (New York: Alfred A. Knopf, 1968), p. 116.

83 Ibid., p. 116.

84 *The Origins of Psychoanalysis. Letters to Wilhelm Fliess, 1887-1902.* Ed. Marie Bonaparte, Anna Freud, Ernst Kris (New York: Basic Books, 1954), p. 119.

85 Quoted in Bernard Muldworf. *Freud* (Paris: Les Editeurs Francais Réunis, 1976), p. 19.

86 Henry Miller, "Psychoanalysis: A Clinical Perspective," *Freud: The Man, his World, his Influence*, ed. Jonathan Miller (London: Weidenfeld & Nicholson, 1972), p. 120.

87 Anthony Quinton, "Freud and Philosophy," *Freud: The Man, his World, his Influence*, p. 79.

88 F. Alexander and S. T. Selesnick, "Freud-Bleuler Correspondence," *Archives of General Psychiatry* 12 (1965), pp. 1-9.

Conclusion

No single law can explain why some artists destroy their works while others, faced with nearly equivalent difficulties, do not. Any study of destructive behavior and of the reasons leading to it must deal with many individual cases. Each of these is very special and very particular—an aggregate of common elements rarely recurring in the same configuration. In each there are many variables and many unpredictable, unique circumstances.

Obviously many artists destroy their work because they consider it a failure. They believe that they have not brought it to the state of perfection they wanted to reach. At times they feel that the work doesn't have a life of its own, or isn't worthy of the artist's oeuvre because, for one reason or another, it doesn't represent his or her best effort. Sometimes, although an artist has put forth his best effort, the results persuade him otherwise. At times an artist may suspect that he cannot do much better than what he has already done, but he proceeds to destroy his work anyhow. He may find a work either repetitive or facile, or merely a failed experiment. Since many artists are never completely satisfied with their work, they must decide whether the work's good points outweigh its bad ones. Even that decision is not always easy. Michel Butor, for example, recently stated that a work is finished when he feels there is simply nothing more he can do to it. This is his criterion for deciding whether or not to send it to the publisher.[1]

Paul Valéry once said that he would rather write a mediocre poem all his own than a masterpiece inspired by the Muses. If this view is not typical of most artists, it underscores the uneasiness of many. Inspired or not, they fear that they themselves are not the masters of the process of artistic creation or of its results. They often sense that this process evolves, unfolding when they are not conscious of its various stages. They are left with the impression that they do not fully understand, much less control, the process. When artists are powerless, or listless and uninspired, or in doubt as to their capacity to give form to an inner vision, they may seek access to some subconscious inner source. But unfortunately, if an artist feels the presence of a hidden or unconscious self that he does not fully understand, he may think that he has been taken over by an outside force which dominates him to excess; it controls him instead of his controlling it.

Artists like Valéry want to control both the work and the process which gives it birth. De Kooning recently told an interviewer: "The structure of a painting should be something that you can't interfere with."[2]   Many artists want to create a structure over which they have total control, one so solidly founded that it gives them an assurance of firmness or incontrovertibility.   But such a sense of exercising complete control is usually short lived, and the artist soon realizes that the work could have turned out very differently.   De Kooning and many others want to produce works that give the appearance of finality, as if such works were born of necessity; "the structure that you can't interfere with" is supposed to be a guarantee of that.   Daniel Albright summarizes the opinion of many artists when he states that a literary work "must have the impossible appearance of being an ordained whole, as if it somehow pre-existed before the writing."[3]

The psychological necessity that a work "have the appearance of being an ordained whole" has probably been the most important factor contributing to the belief in "an inner concept." Without the existence of such a notion about an intuitive vision in their imagination, artists—and critics probably more than artists—might have had great difficulty in understanding the artistic process. But creators know in fact that the idea of the work being a "pre-existent ordained whole" is false.   Valéry pointed this out very clearly when he wrote that creative activity involves the passage from disorder to order and the use of the arbitrary to attain apparent necessity.   The French painter Bazaine (born 1904) states that painters create their work while being led, in a way not clear to them, by a violent sensation that defies verbal articulation.   They are impelled by such things as the brushstrokes they have put down on the canvas.   Bazaine believed that the painter's intelligence enables him to control the work once it is underway, but that this same intelligence is useless to him in foreseeing or initiating the work.[4]   Georges Braque once wrote that in art the only important things were those which could not be explained. He noted that explanations and definitions are bad insofar as they substitute themselves "for the real thing."[5] While Braque was speaking of the work of art, it is likely that he felt the same way about the creative process.

Artists know that works of art do not proceed from a concept, but that they must look as if they did when finished. It is unlikely that they ever look that way to them, even if they do to others. Many artists are provided with what one writer, Pierre-Jean Jouve, calls "an inner demon," whose role it is "to fill them with doubt about the work and negate it as it is being created."[6] The artist can never be sure that he will not be convinced by the doubts and negations of the inner demon. Apparently some artists manage to forget its existence, at least to the extent that they "remember" the inner vision or "inner concept" for their work after having created it.

To fight off "the inner demon," artists want to control their work, but they must also feel that, to a certain extent, it resists them and acquires a life of its own. If this happens, they may no longer be in control, but on the other hand they have the satisfaction that the work is not arbitrary, having acquired an internal necessity of its own. The work then challenges the artist; he does not feel that it is a gratuitous product of his whim or that he has proceeded arbitrarily. The inner or autonomous life that a work acquires in spite of the artist, is a phenomenon that has been felt mainly by writers, although it is not uncommon among other artists such as sculptors, musicians and painters.

Very often, artists have destroyed the immediacy, the spontaneity, and the authenticity of their first impressions by thinking about their experience or analyzing it. It was the fear of analysis which caused Manet to say that the only true thing was to reproduce on first attempt what you see. For this reason, many artists believe that they must develop their skills to such a degree as to sketch, draw, and paint without thinking about what they have seen or analyzing it too much. They know instinctively that conceptualizing prevents a direct grasp of what they have felt because it deforms insight, intuition and feeling, which must remain spontaneous and unretouched. It is likely that this was one of the reasons Cézanne and Monet destroyed many of their canvases.

Both painters believed that the reality they sought to capture, "le motif," was so unstable that they would never be able to fix it on canvas to their satisfaction. They are not the only examples of artists who torment themselves with anxiety that the hand isn't fast enough, and that their colors and paints are inadequate. If they are writers or poets, they will fear that language is not rich, subtle or exact enough, and will lament its limits.

Artists sometimes feel powerless not because they cannot grasp Nature, but because they sense they will not be able to infuse into their creations what they perceive within themselves and which does *not* exist in Nature. Artists such as Wordsworth, Proust, Monet and Cézanne knew that exterior reality provoked in them feelings which were very personal or individual. If they did not give them form, these sensations would be lost forever, at least to them. Cézanne stated that although others felt and saw the same things he did, they didn't have the courage to struggle to express them. He added: " . . . ils font de la peinture de Salon." (They produce Salon paintings).[7] Such artists took the easy way out, catering to prevailing tastes.

Artists have often expressed the view that there is a duality, a masculine and a feminine element in their art; these polarities cannot always be reconciled. Thus Gustav Mahler wrote:

> . . . the artist represents the feminine element opposing the genius that fertilizes him, giving himself entire, carrying the seed in his inmost being, nourishing it as it comes to maturity, until the completed work can be born in the light.[8]

Proust noted in the *Cahier 1908* that "our work makes mothers of us." Such thoughts sometimes cause artists to feel estranged from and unsure of themselves, as if split into mutually uncomprehending personalities. They have within themselves the need to reconcile contradictory principles, or at least opposing ones—an active and a passive.

Artists frequently work without being conscious of what they are doing; Mahler for one, observed that some passages of his work gave him the impression that he had not written them. On occasion, Keats claimed to have been surprised by what he wrote, as if it were the work of another person.[9] The painter Emil Nolde also stated that the best things he had done came as complete surprises to him.[10]

In this connection, Kleist's story, "The Marquise of 0," may well be an allegory of the creative process. The Marquise, having been raped while unconscious, gives birth to a child. Other attempts to find its father having proved unsuccessful, she places an ad in the newspaper asking the father of the child to reveal his identity. In the same way the artist, impregnated by an ecstatic vision, creates without understanding how the work came about. Then he looks for a principle or explanation for what took place within him, igniting the creative spark. However, if an artist does not have what Rimbaud calls the understanding of his visions, he may well decide that his work is imperfect and destroy it.

While some artists believe that their work contains an inner principle which resists them, others need obstacles in order to produce anything worthwhile. Mahler wrote that if his life flowed as smoothly as a river in a meadow, he would no longer be able to write music. The late critic Frank O'Hara, who was at one time director of the Museum of Modern Art and a friend of many contemporary painters, observed that Franz Kline directed all his efforts toward solving problems he encountered in his art; he did not attempt to achieve perfection. When Kline could not find problems he created them.[11] A similar remark about the need to create problems when none existed was also made with regard to Michelangelo by the critic Mariani.

Very frequently artists consider their work an experiment and are not primarily interested in the final product. This was the case with Cézanne, Giacometti and Degas. At the age of sixty-five, after a lifetime of tireless effort, Cézanne said that he made progress every day in his art and that was what he considered most important. Valéry reports that Degas, at the age of seventy, stated that the important thing for an artist was not what he did today but what he would be able to do tomorrow.

Because of the importance they accord to experimentation,—an antidote against rigidity and formulaic repetition—many artists need "to think against themselves." They feel a need to question their taste and their methods, which in turn leads many to destroy their work. Although experiments are essential, the results of these experiments do not necessarily deserve to survive. Often artists destroy their work because they do not want to be limited by what they have done. They are apprehensive that their *oeuvre* might limit their possibilities and throw up a barrier to further progress. It might tempt them to repeat what they have previously done successfully. The poet Pierre Reverdy wrote that an artist secretes his work like a mollusc secretes its shell, to protect himself, and then cannot get out as it has become his prison as well as his armor.[12] Alberto

Giacometti also thought that a finished work had about it a final, unchangeable quality which imprisoned him and blocked him from going on to do other things. For these reasons many artists like to keep a distance between themselves and their work, so as not to become too attached to it. It was most likely for this reason that Chagall, when asked "Are you Marc Chagall?" by a younger painter, replied: "A little."[13]

In addition to the limitations of particular media, to lack of imaginative power or fear of losing it, there are many other causes of dissatisfaction—seemingly less important but often leading to destruction of works and sometimes even to suicide.

One of the most frequent causes of artists' dissatisfaction with their work is that they themselves are diminished by physical impairment due to old age, with its attendant problems of blindness, deafness, arthritis, shaking of the hands, failing strength and memory. All of this is paradoxically tied to the fact that many artists have done their best work when they were old. Of course, artists who reach old age have a field of experience, a maturity, an understanding and a technical mastery which few of their younger colleagues can match. For many, however, physical decline or impairment is felt as a cruel blow, and has prompted some to destroy their work. The most famous example is that of Monet, who continued to paint when his eyesight failed, but who later had large portions of his work from this period burned. Some artists, frustrated by their diminished powers, commit suicide. They do not want to go on with a life devoid of meaning. There is good reason to believe that the suicides of Hemingway and Henry de Montherlant (in 1972) were caused in large part by such instances of "burn-out."

It is also worth noting that artists who destroy their work do not commit suicide and that those who do, do not destroy their works. The most notable exception is Heinrich von Kleist, who destroyed most of the manuscript of one of his plays, and killed himself several years later. His most recent biographer stated that the first action was done "in self-destructive fury like a sulking child," while the second was due to Kleist's "innate suicidal urge."[14] The playwright took out his destructive tendencies on the play he was writing but did so to punish himself and not because the play was in any way irremediably deficient. And although Kleist apparently wanted to rival Aeschylus, Sophocles and Shakespeare, there is no indication that he destroyed his drama because he felt he had not achieved the excellence of his illustrious predecessors.[15]

Balzac's well known view that artistic creation exhausts the artist does not have very wide applicability. Most artists have been so challenged by their work that they have willingly made enormous sacrifices for it, pursuing it with utter single-mindedness. This brings them great satisfaction even when the results are disappointing. Most have been able to renew their emotional and intellectual stamina, as their ceaseless reworking of their pieces shows. And though many become extremely discouraged at one time or another, often their point of view changes quickly if they can confide in sympathetic listeners. The latter have often played an important role in encouraging their artist friends, sympathizing with them, and offering criticism. Examples of this are the supportive understanding given by Max Brod to Kafka, by Gide to Martin du Gard, and Bouilhet to Flaubert. Many other instances could be cited. Artists who have not had close friends have often managed to find strength within themselves and from the support and esteem of their public, even a limited one. Because of their discipline, self-mastery, and understanding of themselves and others, not to mention the freedom their art gave them, few, one suspects, would have exchanged their situation with anyone else's.

Cézanne, Monet, Soutine, Dukas, Giacometti and others destroyed works they thought unworthy of them. These artists had extremely high standards. They wanted their *oeuvre* fit to enter into a canon and take its place in the tradition of what Cézanne called "the art of the museums."

Cézanne thought that influences must be rejected by artists: "We have to give the image of what we see and forget everything that was done before us."[16] This is a common feeling among artists of the nineteenth and twentieth centuries especially, when great importance has been placed on originality. The "shadow of the past" has been feared as a contaminating element preventing the emergence of what is unique and original. While Cézanne knew that he had to find his place in tradition, he must also have known that it included artists who could not be compared to one another and whose work is incommensurate because of its uniqueness. Malraux and others have pointed out that artists have no way of establishing their originality except by rejecting the work of others and proceeding as if no other artists had ever existed. But the problems the creative individual faces are always different from those of predecessors or contemporaries.

Originality is what most artists prized above all else. Henry James believed that an artist's sole justification was "to lend something to a thing." He saw the artist as a shaper, a giver of form, an interpreter. It is the artist who orders reality and makes sense of its myriad appearances. Only an artist with an imaginative vision can do this. Only he can create a meaning previously invisible to the layman. It is his contribution which gives meaning to the things around us. James also spoke of the "incompleteness" of life which comes of not creating anything. For Flaubert, Cézanne, Gauguin, Proust, Monet, Soutine, Giacometti and Musil, art was their very *raison d'être*: nothing else had the importance they single-mindedly gave to their work.

Victor Shklovksi believed that in art a new form appears not to express a new content but to replace an older form which has lost its esthetic value. Artists like Proust, James, Cézanne, Monet and Soutine, however, were convinced that art derives its worth solely from the fact that an artist expresses what is uniquely his. Each believed that if he did not create his work, something would be lost forever, as only he could bring it forth. Because he strongly believes this, Proust's narrator suffers the deep anguish that he may lose in the race against time. Cézanne also thought of originality as the essence of art. He said that his superiority over other artists was that he dared to do what they did not—paint things as he saw them. But this did not prevent him from being unsure about the nature of his originality. The painter who more than any other changed our way of seeing was afraid that he had only "une petite sensation," and that Gauguin, for one, might steal it from him.

Artists have great difficulty in reconciling their individuality, non-conformism and rebelliousness,—their need to express their difference, in short—with their wish to equal the masters and find a place within tradition. To find his place, an artist must create a work with a significance or importance beyond his own immediate world. A very personal and unique element must be presented in such a way that it be recognized as one in a series of works that are of universal interest. Too great an emphasis on originality may cause artists to create excessively narrow and introspective works. This emphasis on originality may lead an artist into uncharted territory. He will grope about, get lost and have to find his way with little help from anyone, except for the encouragement of one or two people. Many artists do not clearly understand what their originality is or consists of. They experiment ceaselessly, with, often enough, wholesale destruction of their own work. Others are afraid to become prisoners of working in too narrow a vein. Still others (Kafka is the most notable example) are frightened by their originality, and by their work. They feel both a repulsion toward it and a compulsion to continue it.

Often artists do not apprehend their originality partly because "the force of originality lies in the unconscious" (l'inconscience).[17] They cannot see the repetitive element in their art and often are incapable of renewing it. Often they come to feel limited by the originality they cannot control so it is not surprising that, irritated by limitations they cannot understand, they chafe and strain, locked in a struggle with a part of themselves. There are, of course, those who can combine "totally mastered acquired knowledge with free-flowing inspiration," to the point that it is impossible to distinguish the two elements.[18] In an article on Bach's *B Minor Mass*, Dukas discusses his great predecessor's way of blending these two elements and notes he had attained a rare degree of perfection. He speaks as if what he terms free-flowing inspiration was the same thing as originality. Neither can be controlled by the artist. Each comes forth mysteriously when an unknown impulse flows or surges into the mind. The element of originality emerges precisely because each creative individual filters inspiration in his own distinctive way. There is no way of predicting how an artist will be able to blend the acquired knowledge of his craft with his creative impulse.

When Dukas states that the force of originality lies in the unconscious, he clearly implies that if the artist were conscious of his originality he would in fact be a craftsman knowing exactly what he was doing. He would then plan, prepare and plot everything down to the last detail. But in that case his originality would be greatly diminished. Art must necessarily have an unpredictable, unrepeatable component. Artists find it difficult to rely exclusively on models, inner or exterior, because in so doing they lose the spontaneous, unpredictable and unique elements which arise from the chance permutations of the creative impulse. The creator must struggle with an obstacle either within himself, in his subject, or in the materials he works with. Theoretically, an artist can attain mastery of his medium. But in the other two domains this mastery is much harder to achieve, which is all to the good: without total mastery he faces a healthy

challenge. In his attempt to meet it, he will draw upon more resources than he is aware of.

We have reviewed the case of Kafka, whose originality
was as much a hindrance as a help to the artist. He feared the
uniqueness of his work, judging it of no interest because what he
presented was too marginal or abnormal. Wordsworth too believed that the poems dealing with events of his own life should
not be published in his lifetime, and could only be justified if
counterbalanced by other works of philosophical merit. He believed the poems dealing with his own, unique situation not suf-
ficiently important in themselves. Was this mere modesty on
his part? Wordsworth undervalued and mistrusted his work,
blind to his own originality.

The comments of a witness as knowledgeable as Elie
Faure show that Soutine also undervalued his art. Like Wordsworth, he did not have sufficient confidence in his own originality, which he disparaged to the point of changing his style. He
was often infuriated with himself because he thought he did not
or could not achieve his goals. In spite of his efforts, his work
"escaped" him, taking on a life of its own. Like Kafka, Wordsworth and Dukas, he was at odds with himself and under un-
remitting, self-imposed pressure.

Inevitably, artists equate the original with the uniquely
personal. They may then begin to wonder if their work at its
most personal is too marginal, too excentric, and of scant interest
to others. At times, the more personal the work, the more re-
moved it may seem from the everyday concerns of humanity.
Often artists may feel a need to justify themselves by stating, as
did Proust, that his work was worthwhile insofar as it enabled
his readers to gain a greater insight into themselves. The impli-
cation is, of course, that the novel is less important in itself than
as an instrument for gaining self-knowledge, for the benefit it
can bring its readers.

Clearly, some of the artists we have touched on here were
hesitant about transmitting works expressive of their uniqueness, personal in the extreme. They had to believe their endeavors to be of the utmost importance and worth all the torments they endured. Many artists act as if suffering were a guarantee of artistic value because quite often they have no criteria by
which to evaluate their work. Most believe that it must have
some wider appeal, for, lacking such a belief, the artist would see
his work as a failure. Keats stated that he would continue to

write poetry even if he knew that it would be burned and that nobody would read it (Letter of 27 October, 1818), but this is not a prevalent feeling among artists. A far greater number seek to convince themselves that their work has some universal merit.

Artists frequently have no criterion by which to judge or assess their originality. If they become too conscious of it they grow unsure of themselves, and at a loss to measure its worth. Often they feel no sense of inner satisfaction about anything they create. Their only certainty as to the merit of their work is the "inward voice" Conrad spoke of, a voice often stilled. For many, the criterion for judging their work is the intensity of suffering they have undergone in recovering what is in the depth of their beings. It is as if only by suffering for their art could they assure themselves of its reality, strength, solidity and worth.

The contradiction lived by Flaubert, Kafka, Soutine, Dukas and others was well understood by the sixteen-year-old Rimbaud, who wrote in a famous letter of May 15, 1871 that the song is rarely the conscious work of the artist, and added: "Je est un autre" (I is another). The artist who creates a work is not the same individual as the one who signs it. He is rather another being, who cannot explain to himself how and why he is creative. Rimbaud, of course, went on to say in this letter that the poet had to study and understand his soul: he would accomplish nothing worthwhile if not fully conscious of his originality, or attuned to "the understanding of his visions." This split in the nature of the artist can never be healed. If "I is another," artists' minds are the battlefields of conflicting feelings. It is not surprising then that one part of the creator's personality should wish to destroy what the second has brought forth, since one half of the self does not understand the other. This sense of the duality of the artist was already evident in Vasari's *Lives of the Painters*.

The difficulty modern artists have in understanding their purpose and originality is illustrated by an interesting passage of *La Prisonnière* in which Proust's narrator notes that all the great works of the nineteenth century are "incomplete." He does not explain why he believes this but suggests that nineteenth century artists could not accomplish what they wanted to do. Their works derive their beauty from the artist's self-consciousness in watching himself at work. The beauty is therefore not intrinsic, but "exterior and superior to the work, retroactively imposing upon it a unity and grandeur it does not have."[19] It appears that nineteenth century artists were incapable of creating autonomous works of art and that any value the works have is one superimposed on them from the exterior. The prefaces, postscripts and retrospective insights of their authors give their products real unity. This unity, although exterior and ulterior to the work itself, "unaware of itself, therefore vital and not logical, did not hinder variety or chill execution."

The narrator's theories indicate that Proust himself seemed to have been troubled by the realization that most works are not created from a preconceived plan. They too are products of chance. The creative artist cannot work within a pre-established structure because he needs the liberty to change the scope, shape or direction of his work whenever he thinks it necessary to do so. This, according to Proust's narrator, often provokes concern that the uncertainties, doubts and contradictions he undergoes during the process of creation may be visible in the end product. Also his freedom (or anarchy) of composition—the endless putting in and taking out—may not be justified by an overriding principle of necessity inherent in the work itself. The narrator believes that artistic self-consciousness is the only true principle in artistic creation: it is what gives the work of art its value. He does not say, however, whether this self-awareness extends to the unconscious.

Cézanne once said that artists must forget everything done before them, and Proust felt that all artists are in the same situation as Homer while composing his epics. These remarks show the a-historical nature of their thought. Precisely because they feel originality to be the essential characteristic of a work, historical considerations and precedents are of little or no use to them. They believe with so many other creators, that they must probe their own inner space, which by definition is different from any other. The example of others, therefore, cannot help; the circumstances are too divergent to be comparable. To add to their problems, many artists feel that they must distrust whatever they do, and think against themselves, to avoid becoming prisoners of their own subjectivity and a set, or formulaic, style.

Often artists are tormented by what they believe to be the meagerness of their inspiration and originality. Duchamp was undoubtedly echoing the fears of many when he said that, for a great artist, "there are only four or five things that really count in his life. The rest is just every-day filler."[20] If this is true, or is perceived to be true by artists, their anxiety about the originality of their work is understandable. The sacrifices they make must seem out of all proportion to the quantity, if not the quality, of original works they produce.

Many artists sense that they can be original only when they are completely themselves. But for so many "being oneself" is so difficult as to be impossible. Monet stated that the older he got, the more fully he realized that artists never dare to express frankly what they feel. He did not elaborate on this remark. Apparently, as Valéry pointed out, artists often sense that something within them inhibits the expression of what they consider most essential. They cannot overcome this inhibiting factor and cannot understand the working of the subconscious. Valéry noted: "Something in us, before us, chooses, eliminates, paralyzes what is possible." Monet appears to agree, and implies that the artist has to fight some obscure part of himself which acts as a barrier to self-expression.

Perhaps those artists who don't appreciate their own originality and who destroy their work are prey to the idea that something deep within themselves prevents them from attaining the knowledge they seek. Like Cézanne, some believe that originality lies precisely in the attempt to perceive the meaning of themselves through their art. This thought was also expressed by Malraux, who wrote that art is by definition original. He remarks that modern artists must be conscious of their originality and must see the fundamental difference which makes them stand out: here lies the very expression of their originality. But as we know, artists want to comprehend the reasons for their difference, the mechanics behind their originality. They do not want to be sorcerers' apprentices, apprised of only one half of the formula for accomplishing their task. But, when all is said and done, there is no reason to believe that artists are any nearer to an understanding of their individuality than they have ever been. As we have said before, it is perhaps the search for such understanding that leads them to persevere in their work.

Probably the most succinct and accurate statement about artists' lives was made by the novelist protagonist of Henry James' "The Middle Years," who states: "We work in the dark—we do what we can—we give what we have. Our doubt is our passion and our passion is our task. The rest is the madness of art."

Notes

[1] "Les Modifications de Michel Butor: Entretien avec Antoine de Gaudemar," *Magazine Littéraire*, no. 191, janvier 1983, p. 84.

[2] Avis Berman, "Willem de Kooning," *Art News*, February 1982, p. 71.

[3] Daniel Albright, *Representation and the Imagination* (Chicago; Chicago University Press, 1981), p. 165.

[4] Quoted in Noël Mouloud, *La Peinture et l'espace* (Paris: Presses Universitaires de France, 1964), p. 199.

[5] Quoted in John Russell, *The Meaning of Modern Art* (New York: Museum of Modern Art, 1981), p. 281.

[6] Pierre-Jean Jouve, "Six lettres à Claude Le Maguet," *Nouvelle Revue Francaise*, nos. 366-367, juillet-août 1983, p. 282.

[7] Quoted in John Rewald, *The History of Impressionism*, 4th ed. (New York: Museum of Modern Art, 1973), p. 246.

[8] Quoted in Henri de la Grange, *Mahler* (New York: Doubleday & Co., 1973), p. 274.

[9] See Henri de la Grange, *Mahler*, p. 368. See Amy Lowell, *John Keats*, 2 vols. (Cambridge, Mass.: Houghton-Mifflin - The Riverside Press, 1925), I, 501-502.

[10] Martin Urban, "Emil Nolde," *Art and Artists*, July 1970, p. 48.

[11] Frank O'Hara, *Art Chronicles 1954-1966* (New York: George Braziller, 1975), p. 46.

[12] Quoted in M. D. Philippe, *L'Activité Artistique*, I, p. 359.

[13] Marek Halter, *Le Fou et les rois* (Paris: Albin-Michel, 1979), p. 133.

[14] Robert E. Helbling, *The Major Works of Heinrich von Kleist* (New York: New Directions, 1975), pp. 11-12.

[15] Ilse Graham, *Heinrich von Kleist, Word into Flesh: A Poet's Quest for the Symbol* (Berlin, New York: Walter de Gruyter, 1977), p. 260.

[16] Quoted in Bernard Dorival, *Cézanne* (Paris: Editions Pierre Tisné, 1948), p. 103.

[17] Paul Dukas, *Chroniques musicales sur deux siècles, 1882-1932*, p. 28.

[18] Ibid., p. 28.

[19] Marcel Proust, *A la rercherche du temps perdu*, III, 160-161. An excellent discussion of this passage can be found in Leo Bersani, *From Balzac to Beckett* (New York: Oxford University Press, 1970).

[20] Quoted by Pierre Cabanne, *Dialogues with Marcel Duchamp* (New York: Viking Press, 1971), p. 69.

BIBLIOGRAPHY

Abrams, M. H. NATURAL SUPERNATURALISM: TRADITION AND REVO-LUTION IN ROMANTIC LITERATURE. New York: Norton, 1971.

Abrams, M. H. "The Prelude as the Portrait of an Artist." *Bicentenary Words-worth Studies in Memory of John Finch.* Ithaca, N.Y.: Cornell University Press, 1970, pp. 180-237.

Albright, Daniel. REPRESENTATION AND THE IMAGINATION. Chicago: The University of Chicago Press, 1981.

Alexander, F., S. T. Selesnick. "Freud-Bleuler Correspondence." *Archives of General Psychiatry* 12 (1965), pp. 1-9.

Alvarez, Alfred. THE SAVAGE GOD. New York: Random House, 1972.

Ashbrook, William. "The Two Faces of Boito." *Opera News*, April 10, 1976, pp. 12-15.

Asselineau, Roger. "Ernest Hemingway." *Encyclopaedia Universalis*, IX, 1985, pp. 193-195.

Backus, Susan. Boito's Unfinishable *Nerone*." *Opera Journal*, XIV, no. 3, 1981, pp. 17-26.

Balzac, Honoré de. LA COMÉDIE HUMAINE. 12 vols. Paris: Gallimard-Pléiade, 1976-1981.

——. LETTRES Á MADAME HANSKA. 4 vols. Paris: Editions du Delta, 1967.

——. OEUVRES COMPLETES. 24 vols. Paris: Club de l'honnête homme, 1956.

Bardèche, Maurice. L'OEUVRE DE FLAUBERT. Paris: Les Sept Couleurs, 1974.

——. MARCEL PROUST ROMANCIER. Paris: Les Sept Couleurs, 1971.

Beardsley, Monroe C. AESTHETICS: PROBLEMS IN THE PHILOSOPHY OF CRITICISM. New York: Harcourt, Brace & World, Inc., 1958.

Berman, Avis. "Willem de Kooning: I am only halfway through." *Art News*, February 1982, pp. 68-73.

Bernard, Emile. SOUVENIRS SUR PAUL CÉZANNE ET LETTRES. Paris: A la Renovation esthétique, 1920.

Bernard, Emile. "Souvenirs sur Paul Cézanne et lettres inédites." *Mercure de France*, 1er octobre 1907, pp. 385-404; 16 octobre 1907, pp. 606-627.

Bersani, Leo. FROM BALZAC TO BECKETT. New York: Oxford University Press, 1970.

Blanchot, Maurice. "Kafka et Brod." *Nouvelle Revue Française*, octobre 1954, pp. 695-707.

———. "Robert Musil." *Nouvelle Revue Française*, février 1958, pp. 301-309; mars 1958, pp. 479-490.

———. "Proust." *Nouvelle Revue Française*, août 1954, pp. 286-294; septembre 1954, pp. 479-487.

Bordier, Roger. L'OBJET CONTRE L'ART. Paris: Hachette, 1972.

Breton, André. LE POINT DU JOUR. Paris: Gallimard, 1970.

Brinkley, Roberta Florence. COLERIDGE ON THE SEVENTEENTH CENTURY. New York: Greenwood Press Publishers, 1968.

Butor, Michel. "Les Modifications de Michel Butor: Entretien avec Antoine de Gaudemar." *Magazine Littéraire*, no. 191, janvier 1983, pp. 80-85.

Cabanne, Pierre. DIALOGUES WITH MARCEL DUCHAMP. Trans. Ron Padgett. New York: The Viking Press, 1971.

Castaing, Marcelin, Jean Leymarie. SOUTINE. Trans. John Ross. New York: Harry N. Abrams, 1962.

Céline, L. F. "L. F. Céline." Interview with J. Darribehaude, J. Guenot, André Parinaud, Claude Sarraute. *Writers at Work*, 3rd series. New York: The Viking Press, 1967, pp. 86-102.

Chabot, Georges. HOMMAGE TO GEORGES ROUAULT. New York: Tudor Publishing Co., 1971.

Chapon, François. OEUVRE GRAVÉ DE ROUAULT. Texte de François Chapon. 2 vols. Catalogue établi par Isabelle Rouault avec la collaboration d'Olivier Nouaille-Rouault. Monte-Carlo: Editions André Sautet, 1973.

Charbonnier, Georges. "Entretien avec Alberto Giacometti." *Le Monologue du peintre*, vol. 1. Paris: Julliard, 1959, pp. 159-170.

Charbonnier, Georges. LE MONOLOGUE DU PEINTRE. 2 vols. Paris: Julliard, 1959.

Charensol, Georges. GEORGES ROUAULT, L'HOMME ET L'OEUVRE. Paris: Editions des quatre chemins, 1926.

Chastel, André. L'IMAGE DANS LE MIROIR. Collection Idées. Paris: Gallimard, 1980.

Clay, Jean. VISAGES DE L'ART MODERNE. Lausanne: Editions Rencontre, 1969.

Cogniat, Raymond. SOUTINE. Trans. Eileen B. Hennessy. New York: Crown Publishers, 1973.

Colliée, Andrée. "Souvenirs sur Soutine." *Le Spectacle des Arts*, décembre 1944, p. 17-18.

Conrad, Joseph. THE COLLECTED LETTERS OF JOSEPH CONRAD. Ed. F. R. Karl, L. Davis. New York: Cambridge University Press, 1983.

——. LETTERS TO WILLIAM BLACKWOOD AND DAVID S. MELDRUM. Ed. William Blackburn. Durham, N. C.: Duke University Press, 1958.

Costigan, Giovanni. FREUD: A SHORT BIOGRAPHY. New York: MacMillan, 1965.

Courthion, Pierre. GEORGES ROUAULT. New York: Harry N. Abrams, 1962.

Courthion, Pierre. "Rouault au Louvre." *Arts, Lettres, Spectacles*, 24-30 juin 1964, p. 9.

——. SOUTINE, PEINTRE DU DÉCHIRANT. Lausanne: Edita-Denoël, 1972.

Coutot, Maurice. "L'Affaire Rouault." *Gazette des Beaux-Arts*, avril 1974, Supplément, p. 2.

Darlington, Beth. "Preface." William Wordsworth: *Home at Grasmere*. Ed. Beth Darlington. Ithaca, N.Y.: Cornell University Press, 1977, pp. ix-xii.

——. "Introduction." William Wordsworth: *Home at Grasmere*. Ed. Beth Darlington. Ithaca, N.Y.: Cornell University Press, 1977, pp. 3-32.

Delacroix, Eugène. JOURNAL. 3 vols. Paris: Plon, 1895.

Descargues, Pierre. "Rouault a gagné son procès." *Arts, Lettres, Spectacles*, 21 mars 1947, pp. 1,3.

Dorival, Bernard. CÉZANNE. Paris: Tisné, 1948.

Dorival, Bernard. "Préface." Georges Rouault. *Oeuvres inachevées données à l'Etat*. Exposition Musée du Louvre, juin-novembre 1964. Paris: Consorts Rouault, 1964, pp. 11-19.

Du Bos, Charles. APPROXIMATIONS. Paris: Fayard, 1965.

Du Bos, Charles. "Jacques Rivière." *Approximations*. Paris: Fayard, 1965, pp. 459-503.

Dukas, Paul. CHRONIQUES MUSICALES SUR DEUX SIECLES 1892-1932. Paris: Stock, 1980.

——. CORRESPONDANCE DE PAUL DUKAS. Ed. Georges Favre. Paris: Editions Durand et Cie., 1971.
Dumayet, Pierre. VU ET ENTENDU. Paris: Stock, 1964.

Dunlop, Ian. THE SHOCK OF THE NEW. New York: American Heritage Press, 1972.

Dupin, Jacques. ALBERTO GIACOMETTI. Paris: Maeght, 1962.

Durrell, Lawrence. "Lawrence Durrell." Interview with Julian Mitchell, Gene Andrewski. *Writers at Work*, 2nd series. New York: The Viking Press, 1963, pp. 259-282.

Ellenberger, Henri. THE DISCOVERY OF THE UNCONSCIOUS: THE HISTORY AND EVOLUTION OF DYNAMIC PSYCHIATRY. New York: Basic Books, 1970.

Favre, Georges. L'OEUVRE DE PAUL DUKAS. Paris: Durand et Cie., 1969.

Flaubert, Gustave. CORRESPONDANCE. 11 vols. Paris: Conard-Lambert, 1926-1944.

Flinker, Martin. "Mes souvenirs de Robert Musil." *Robert Musil:* Cahiers de L'Herne, no. 41. Ed. Marie-Louise Roth, Robert Olmi. Paris: L'Herne, 1981, pp. 277-281.

Frances, Robert. PSYCHOLOGIE DE L'ESTHÉTIQUE. Paris: Presses Universitaires de France, 1968.

Freud, Sigmund. THE STANDARD EDITION OF THE COMPLETE PSYCHOLOGICAL WORKS OF SIGMUND FREUD. Trans. ed. James Strachey et al. 24 vols. London: Hogarth Press, 1953-1974.

Freud, Sigmund. THE LETTERS OF SIGMUND FREUD. Trans. Tania and James Stern. Ed. Ernst L. Freud. New York: Basic Books, 1960.

——. THE ORIGINS OF PSYCHOANALYSIS. LETTERS TO WILHELM FLIESS, 1887-1902. Ed. Marie Bonaparte, Anna Freud, Ernst Kris. New York: Basic Books, 1954.

Garcin, Jérôme. "Romain Gary." *1981 Encyclopaedia Universalis*. Paris: Encyclopaedia Universalis, 1982, pp. 551-552.

Gasquet, Joachim. CÉZANNE. Paris, 1921.

Gauguin, Paul. LETTERS TO HIS WIFE AND FRIENDS. Ed. Maurice Mal-
    ingue. Trans. Henry J. Stenning. Cleveland: World Publishing Co.,
    1949.

———. LETTERS TO AMBROISE VOLLARD AND ANDRÉ FONTAINAS. Ed.
    John Rewald. San Francisco: The Grabhorn Press, 1943.

———. LETTRES A ANDRE FONTAINAS. Paris, 1921.

———. 45 LETTRES A VINCENT, THEO ET JO VAN GOGH. Introduction Doug-
    las Cooper. Lausanne: La Bibliothèque des Arts, 1983.

Gauthier-Vignal. PROUST CONNU ET INCONNU. Paris: Editions Robert
    Laffont, 1976.

Genette, Gérard. FIGURES I. Paris: Le Seuil, 1966.

George, Waldemar, Geneviève Nouaille-Rouault. L'UNIVERS DE ROUAULT.
    Paris: Scrépel, 1971.

Gide, André, Roger Martin du Gard. CORRESPONDANCE. 2 vols. Paris:
    Gallimard, 1968.

Glatzer, Nahum. "Introduction." I Am a Memory Come Alive. Ed. Nahum
    Glatzer. New York Schocken Books, 1974, pp. vii-xiii.

Glueck, Grace. "Scenes from a marriage: Krasner and Pollock." Art News,
    December 1981, pp. 57-61.

Goldaine, Louis, Pierre Astier. CES PEINTRES VOUS PARLENT. Paris:
    L'Oeil du temps, 1964.

Gordon, Donald E. "Ernst Ludwig Kirchner: By Instinct Possessed." Art in
    America, November 1980, pp. 81-95.

Graham, Ilse. Heinrich von Kleist, WORD INTO FLESH: A POET'S QUEST
    FOR THE SYMBOL. Berlin, New York: Walter de Gruyter, 1977.

Grandville, Frederic de la; Marc Vignal. "Paul Dukas." Larousse de la
    Musique, vol. 1. Paris: Larousse, 1982, p. 490.

Grange, Henri-Louis de la. MAHLER. Vol I. New York: Doubleday, 1973.

Greenberg, Clement. "Chaim Soutine." Partisan Review, no. 1, January-Febru-
    ary 1951, pp. 82-87.

Grenier, Jean. ENTRETIENS AVE DIX-SEPT PEINTRES NON-FIGURATIFS.
    Paris: Calmann-Lévy, 1965.

Groth, Gerda Michaelis (Mademoiselle Garde). MES ANNÉES AVEC SOU-
TINE. Paris: Denoël, 1973.

Gualerzi, Giorgio. "Nerone." *Opera*, November 1975, pp. 1065-1066.

Guston, Philip. "Faith, Hope and Impossibility." *Art News Annual*, 1966, pp.
101-103, 152-153.
Halter, Marek. Le Fou et les rois. Paris: Albin-Michel, 1979.

Hartman, Georffrey. WORDSWORTH'S POETRY 1787-1814. New Haven:
Yale University Press, 1964.

Helbling, Robert. THE MAJOR WORKS OF HEINRICH VON KLEIST. New
York: New Directions, 1975.

Hess, Thomas. "Alberto Giacometti: The Uses of Adversity." *Art News*, May
1958, pp. 34-35, 67.

———. "Alberto Giacometti - 1901-1966." *Art News*, March 1966, p. 35.

Holt, Elizabeth G. A DOCUMENTARY HISTORY OF ART. Princeton: Princeton University Press, 1982.

Hopkins, G. W. "Paul Dukas." *The New Grove Dictionary of Music and Musicians.* Ed. Stanley Sadie. New York: MacMillan, 1980, vol. II, pp. 863-
867.

Hoffman, Werner. "Marcel Duchamp and Emblematic Realism." *Marcel
Duchamp in Perspective.* Ed. Joseph Masheck. Englewood Cliffs, N.J.:
Prentice Hall, Inc., 1975, pp. 53-66.

Hoschédé, Jean-Pierre. MONET. 2 vols. Genève: Pierre Cailler, 1960.

Isaacson, Joel. CLAUDE MONET: OBSERVATION AND REFLECTION. New
York: Dutton, 1978.

Jaccottet, Philippe. "Postface." Robert Musil: *L'Homme sans qualités.* vol. II.
Paris: Le Seuil, 1979, pp. 1035-1038.

———. "Introduction." Robert Musil: *Journaux.* 2 vols. Traduit par Phillippe
Jaccottet. Paris: Le Seuil, 1981, pp. 9-19.

Janouch, Gustav. CONVERSATIONS WITH FRANZ KAFKA. New York:
New Directions, 1971.

Jones, Ernest. THE LIFE AND WORK OF SIGMUND FREUD. 2 vols. New
York: Basic Books, 1981.

Jouffroy, Alain. "Alberto Giacometti: Portrait d'un artiste." *Arts, Lettres, Spectacles,* no. 545, 7-13 décembre 1955, p. 9.

Jouve, Pierre-Jean. "Six lettres à Claude Le Maguet." *Nouvelle Revue Française*, numéros 366-367, juillet-août 1983, pp. 278-286.

Jung, C. G. MEMORIES, DREAMS AND REFLECTIONS. Trans. A. and C. Winston. New York: Pantheon Books, 1961.

Kafka, Franz. DEAREST FATHER: STORIES AND OTHER WRITINGS. Trans. Ernst Kaiser and Eithne Wilkins. New York: Schocken Books, 1954.

——. I AM A MEMORY COME ALIVE. Ed. Nahum Glatzer. New York: Schocken Books, 1974.

——. LETTERS TO FELICE. Ed. Erich Heller and Jürgen Born. Trans. James Stern and Elizabeth Duckworth. New York: Schocken Books, 1973.

——. LETTERS TO FRIENDS, FAMILY AND EDITORS. Trans. Richard and Clara Winston. New York: Schocken Books, 1977.

Klein, John. "The Enigma of Boito." *Opera*, March 7, 1968, pp. 191-197.

Kramer, Hilton. THE AGE OF THE AVANT-GARDE. New York: Farrar, Strauss and Giroux, 1973.

Lassaigne, Jacques. DICTIONNAIRE DE LA PEINTURE MODERNE. Ed. Jacques Lassaigne. Paris: Hazan, 1954.

Lassaigne, Jacques. "Rouault." *Dictionnaire de la peinture moderne*. Paris: F. Hazan, 1954, pp. 250-253.

Lebensjtejn, Claude. "Les textes du peintre." *Critique*, no. 324, mai 1974, pp. 400-433.

Leiris, Michel. ALBERTO GIACOMETTI. DESSINS. Galerie Claude Bernard. Paris, 1975.

Lhote, André. LES INVARIANTS PLASTIQUES. MANET ET PICASSO. Paris: Hermann, 1965.

Lord, James. "Alberto Giacometti, sculpteur et peintre." *L'Oeil*, no. 1, janvier 1955, pp. 14-20.

Lord, James. A GIACOMETTI PORTRAIT. New York: Museum of Modern Art, 1965.

Lowell, Amy. JOHN KEATS. 2 vols. Cambridge, Massachusetts: Houghton-Mifflin - The Riverside Press, 1925.

Luft, David. ROBERT MUSIL AND THE CRISIS OF EUROPEAN CULTURE, 1882-1942. Berkeley: University of California Press, 1980.

Mallarmé, Stéphane. OEUVRES. Paris: Gallimard - Pléiade, 1945.

Malraux, André. LES VOIX DU SILENCE: La Psychologie de l'art - Le Musée Imaginaire. Paris: Albert Skira, 1947.

———. L'INTEMPOREL. Paris: Gallimard, 1976.

———. L'IRÉEL. Paris: Gallimard, 1974.

———. PICASSO'S MASK. Trans. June Guicharnaud with Jacques Guicharnaud. New York: Holt, Rhinehart, Winston, 1974.

Marchiori, Giuseppe. ROUAULT. New York: Reynal & Co., William Morrow & Co. n.d.

Martin du Gard, Roger. CORRESPONDANCE GÉNÉRALE. Ed. Maurice Rieuneau. Vol. I (1896-1913). Vol. II (1914-1918). Paris: Gallimard, 1980.

Martin du Gard, Roger. OEUVRES COMPLETES. Paris: Gallimard - Pléiade, 1955.

Masson, André. ÉCRITS. Paris: Hermann, 1976.

Matter, Mercedes. "Giacometti: In the Vicinity of the Impossible." Art News, Summer 1965, pp. 27-31, 53-54.

Maupassant, Guy de. PIERRE ET JEAN, 1888.

Michel, Paul-Henri. "The Lesson of the Renaissance." Diogenes, no. 46, 1964, pp. 25-43.

Miller, Henry. "Psychoanalysis: A Clinical Perspective." Freud: The Man, his World, his Influence. Ed. Jonathan Miller. London: Weidenfeld and Nicholson, 1972, pp. 112-123.

Miller, Jonathan, ed. FREUD: THE MAN, HIS WORLD, HIS INFLUENCE. London: Weidenfeld & Nicholson, 1972.

Mouloud, Noël. LA PEINTURE ET L'ESPACE. Paris: Presses Universitaires de France, 1964.

Musil, Robert. BRIEFE. Ed. Adolf Frisé. Hamburg: Rowohlt, 1976.

———. GESAMMELTE WERKE. 3 vols. Hamburg: Rowohlt, 1952-1957.

———. TAGEBÜCHER, APHORISMEN, ESSAYS UND REDEN. Hamburg: Rowohlt, 1955.

———. L'HOMME SANS QUALITÉS. Traduit par Philippe Jaccottet. 2 vols. Paris: Le Seuil, 1957.

Noyes, Russell. WORDSWORTH. New York: Twayne, 1971.

O'Hara, Frank. ART CHRONICLES 1954-1966. New York: George Braziller, 1975.

Pacht, Otto. "A propos des oeuvres pré-posthumes de Robert Musil." *Robert Musil.* Cahiers de L'Herne, no. 41. Ed. Marie-Louise Roth, Robert Olmi. Paris: L'Herne, 1981, pp. 276-277.

Parinaud, Andre. "Entretien avec Alberto Giacometti - Pourquoi je suis sculpteur." *Arts, Lettres, Spectacles,* no. 873, 13-19 juin 1962, pp. 1, 5.

Pasternak, Boris. "Boris Pasternak." Interview with Olga Carlisle. *Writers at Work.* 2nd series. New York: The Viking Press, 1963, pp. 113-136.

Paulhan, Jean. OEUVRES COMPLETES. 5 vols. Paris: Cercle du Livre précieux, 1970.

Pazmoor, Radiana. "The Librettists." *National Association of Teachers of Singing Bulletin* (NATS), February-March 1974, pp. 16-24.

Perry, Lilla Cabot. "Reminiscences of Claude Monet from 1889 to 1909." *The American Magazine of Art,* XVIII, no. 3, March 1927, pp. 119-125.

Peyret, Jean-Francois. "Musil ou les contradictions de la modernité." *Critique,* no. 339-340, août-septembre 1975, pp. 846-863.

Philippe, M. D. L'ACTIVITÉ ARTISTIQUE. 2 vols. Paris: Editions Beauchesne, 1969-1970.

Pingaud, Bernard. "Omega." *Nouvelle Revue de Psychologie,* no. 14 (1976), pp. 247-260.

Pissarro, Camille. LETTERS TO HIS SON LUCIEN. Ed. John Rewald. 3rd Edition. Mamaroneck, New York: Paul Appel, Publisher, 1972.

Plimpton, George. WRITERS AT WORK. The Paris Review Interview Series. Second Series, Third Series. New York: The Viking Press, 1963, 1967.

Proust, Antonin. SOUVENIRS SUR EDOUARD MANET. Paris: Laurens, 1913.

Proust, Marcel. A LA RECHERCHE DU TEMPS PERDU. Ed. Pierre Clarac and André Ferré. 3 vols. Paris: Gallimard - Pleiade, 1954.

——. CARNET 1908. Ed. Philip Kolb. Paris: Gallimard, 1976.

——. CONTRE SAINTE-BEUVE. Paris: Gallimard - Pléiade, 1971.

——. CORRESPONDANCE. Ed. Philip Kolb. Paris: Plon, 1970——.

Quinton, Anthony. "Freud and Philosophy." *Freud: The Man, his World, his Influence.* Ed. Jonathan Miller. London: Weidenfeld and Nicholson, 1972, pp. 72-83.

Rewald, John. THE HISTORY OF IMPRESSIONISM. 4th Ed. New York: Museum of Modern Art, 1973.

Rieff, Philip. FREUD: THE MIND OF THE MORALIST. New York: Viking Press, 1959.

Roazen, Paul. FREUD: POLITICAL AND SOCIAL THOUGHT. New York: Alfred B. Knopf, 1968.

Robert, Marthe. FROM OEDIPUS TO MOSES. Trans. Ralph Manheim. New York: Anchor Books, 1976.

Robbe-Grillet, Alain. POUR UN NOUVEAU ROMAN. Collection Idées. Paris: Gallimard, 1963.

Roger-Marx, Claude. "Rouault au Louvre." *La Revue de Paris,* août-septembre 1964, pp. 144-145.

Rose, Michael. "The Birth of an Opera." *About the House,* vol. 5, no. 5, Spring 1978, pp. 56-64.

Rosenberg, Harold. THE ANXIOUS OBJECT. New York: Horizon Press, 1966.

Roth, Marie-Louise. ROBERT MUSIL. Ed. Marie-Louise Roth. Paris: Cahiers de L'Herne, 1982.

Rouault, George et André Suarès. CORRESPONDANCE. Paris: Gallimard, 1960.

Rouault, Georges. SUR L'ART ET SUR LA VIE. Préface de Bernard Dorival. Paris: Denoel-Gonthier, 1971.

Russell, John. THE MEANING OF MODERN ART. New York: Museum of Modern Art, 1981.

Sammazeuilh, Gustave. "In Memoriam." *La Revue Musicale,* mai-juin 1936, pp. 52-56.

Sand, George. CORRESPONDANCE. Ed. Georges Lubin. Paris: Garnier, 1964—.

Schneider, Pierre. LOUVRE DIALOGUES. New York: Atheneum, 1971.

Selz, Peter. NEW IMAGES OF MAN. New York: Museum of Modern Art, 1959.

Sicard, Claude. Roger Martin du Gard: LES ANNÉES D'APPRENTISSAGE LITTÉRAIRE-1881-1910. Université Lille III - Honoré Champion, 1976.

Simpson, Eileen. POETS IN THEIR YOUTH. New York: Random House, 1982.

Steegmuller, Francis F. THE LETTERS OF GUSTAVE FLAUBERT 1830-1857. Selected edited and translated by F. F. Steegmuller. Cambridge, Mass.: Harvard University Press, 1979, 1980.

Stone, Peter. "Soutine at Céret." *Art and Artists*, April 1970, pp. 54-57.

Sulloway, Frank J. Freud: BIOLOGIST OF THE MIND. New York: Basic Books, 1979.

Sylvester, David. "The Residue of a Vision." *Alberto Giacometti: Sculpture, Paintings, Drawings, 1913-1965.* London: The Arts Council of Great Britain, 1965, pp. 19-27.

——. "Introduction." *Chaim Soutine.* Tate Gallery, 28 September - 5 November, 1963. London: The Arts Council of Great Britain, 1963, pp. 4-15.

Tomkins, Calvin. OFF THE WALL. New York: Doubleday & Co., Inc., 1980.

Tworkov, Jack. "The Wandering Soutine." *Art News*, November 1950, pp. 30-33, 62.

Urban, Martin. "Emil Nolde." *Art and Artists*, July 1970, pp. 48-51.

Valéry, Paul. OEUVRES. Ed. Jean Hytier. 2 Vols. Paris: Gallimard-Pléiade, 1957-1960.

Valéry, Paul. CAHIERS. 29 Vols. Paris: Centre National de la Recherche Scientifique (CNRS), 1957-1962.

Vallier, Dora. REPERES: LA PEINTURE EN FRANCE, DÉBUT ET FIN D'UN SYSTEME VISUEL, 1870-1970. Paris: Alfieri et Lacroix, 1976.

Verdet, André. ENTRETIENS, NOTES ET ÉCRITS SUR LA PEINTURE. Paris: Galilée, 1978.

Von Einem, Herbert. MICHELANGELO. Trans. Ronald Taylor. London: Methuen, 1973.

Watt, Alexander. "Conversation with Giacometti." *Arts*, no. 4 (1960), pp. 100-102.

Wheeler, Monroe. SOUTINE. New York: Museum of Modern Art, 1950.

——. BONNARD AND HIS ENVIRONMENT. New York: Doubleday & Co., Inc., 1964.

Wildenstein, Daniel. MONET. 3 vols. Lausanne: La Bibliothèque des Arts, 1974-1979.

Woodring, Carl. WORDSWORTH. New York: Houghton-Mifflin, 1965.

Wordsworth, William. THE LETTERS OF WILLIAM AND DOROTHY WORDSWORTH. The Early Years, 1787-1805. Rev. Chester L. Shaver, 2nd Edition. Oxford: Clarendon, 1967.

———. THE LETTERS OF WILLIAM AND DOROTHY WORDSWORTH. The Middle Years, 1806-1811. Rev. Mary Moorman, 2nd Edition. Oxford: Clarendon, 1969.

———. THE LETTERS OF WILLIAM AND DOROTHY WORDSWORTH. The Later Years, 1821-1828. Rev. Alan G. Hill, 2nd Edition. Oxford: Clarendon, 1978.

———. THE LETTERS OF WILLIAM AND DOROTHY WORDSWORTH. The Later Years, 1829-1834. Rev. Alan G. Hill, 2nd Edition. V, part 2. Oxford: Clarendon, 1979.

———. THE PRELUDE. Ed. Jonathan Wordsworth, M. H. Abrams and Stephen Hill. New York: Norton, 1979.

Yanaihara, Isaku. "Pages de Journal." *Derrière le miroir*, mai 1961, pp. 18-26.

Index